FALSEHOOD AND FALLACY

FALSEHOOD AND FALLACY

How to Think, Read, and Write in the Twenty-First Century

Bethany Kilcrease

UNIVERSITY OF TORONTO PRESS

Toronto Buffalo London

ISBN 978-1-4875-8862-5 (cloth) ISBN 978-1-4875-8863-2 (EPUB)
ISBN 978-1-4875-8861-8 (paper) ISBN 978-1-4875-8864-9 (PDF)

Library and Archives Canada Cataloguing in Publication

Title: Falsehood and fallacy : how to think, read, and write in the twenty-first century / Bethany Kilcrease.
Names: Kilcrease, Bethany, author.
Description: Includes bibliographical references and index.
Identifiers: Canadiana (print) 20200412310 | Canadiana (ebook) 20200412388 | ISBN 9781487588625 (cloth) | ISBN 9781487588618 (paper) | ISBN 9781487588632 (EPUB) | ISBN 9781487588649 (PDF)
Subjects: LCSH: Critical thinking. | LCSH: Reading. | LCSH: Academic writing. | LCSH: Research – Methodology. | LCSH: Fallacies (Logic) | LCSH: Truthfulness and falsehood. | LCSH: Information literacy. | LCSH: Electronic information resource literacy.
Classification: LCC BF441 .K55 2021 | DDC 153.4/2—dc23

We welcome comments and suggestions regarding any aspect of our publications – please feel free to contact us at news@utorontopress.com or visit us at utorontopress.com.

Every effort has been made to contact copyright holders; in the event of an error or omission, please notify the publisher.

University of Toronto Press acknowledges the financial assistance to its publishing program of the Canada Council for the Arts and the Ontario Arts Council, an agency of the Government of Ontario.

Canada Council
for the Arts

Conseil des Arts
du Canada

ONTARIO ARTS COUNCIL
CONSEIL DES ARTS DE L'ONTARIO

an Ontario government agency
un organisme du gouvernement de l'Ontario

Funded by the   Financé par le
Government   gouvernement
of Canada   du Canada

Canada

MIX
Paper from
responsible sources
FSC® C016245

In memory of Dr. Brent Chesley and Dr. Mark Hoolihan

CONTENTS

PREFACE

I have now been teaching undergraduate students for over a decade. One consistent thing that I – and I imagine pretty much all instructors – have noticed in my classes is the need for teaching careful attention to source evaluation, reading, and writing. The book you are now holding in your hands began as a now defunct blog that I designed to partially meet this need. In its short life span, my blog, entitled *History Writing Demystified for the Undergraduate Scholar*, included short posts offering advice on topics such as taking notes in class, writing summaries of secondary sources, and recognizing informal logical fallacies. I'm not sure how many students ever read my blog, but University of Toronto Press acquisitions editor Natalie Fingerhut discovered it and asked me to submit a book proposal based on some of its content. From there, writing fresh content commenced, and I'd like to thank several individuals for reading (sometimes very) rough drafts of chapters. These include Julie Bevins, writing center coordinator; Shellie Jeffries, co-director of the Grace Hauenstein Library; Nalana La Framboise, writing consultant; Sarah K. Nytroe, associate professor of history; Molly Patterson, associate professor of political science; Gretchen Rumohr, associate professor of English; Holly Scheer, senior contributor to the Federalist; and Daniel Wagner, assistant professor of philosophy. I would also like to thank my husband, Dr. Jack Kilcrease, for reading several chapters; my daughters, Miriam and Ruth, for not keeping Mommy too busy to write; and the rest of my family.

CHAPTER 1

INTRODUCTION

Remember when Palestinians recognized Texas as a part of Mexico? Do you recall the time when the National Football League decided to fine each of the Pittsburgh Steelers one million dollars for remaining in their locker room during the national anthem? I certainly remember reading about both of these things. After all, based on the number of Google hits, these were among the most widely shared news stories on social media in 2017.[1] Of course, neither of these stories are true. Both originated in explicitly satirical websites.[2] Maine resident Christopher Blair, a man in possession of both a fervid imagination and – at one time – a website called TheLastLineOfDefense.org, published the NFL story. While Blair states that his goal is to use satire "to expose the extreme bigotry and hate and subsequent blind gullibility that festers in right-wing nutjobs," readers often share his stories as real news. Moreover, operators of intentional (as opposed to explicitly satirical) fake news websites, in eastern Europe and elsewhere, often help themselves to content like Blair's and repost it without citation as actual news.[3]

With trolls like Blair hard at work, should you trust what you read? Does it make a difference if the text came from a print book or off the internet? What about from a university's website as opposed to a personal blog? Can you even remember a time before the internet? Do you know that at one time in the hoary past a "face book" was actually a physical paper book published by colleges as a photo directory? Hence the name "Facebook." Did you grow up in a time before the smartphone functioned as a ubiquitous accessory in one's back (or front) pocket? If the answer is no, then you were probably born between the late 1990s and 2010s.[4] Demographers refer to this generation as Generation Z or the Post-Millennial Generation. This generation is stereotypically seen as especially tech savvy, although in our screen-saturated environment, this can be true of students from all generations. Regardless of their generation, my students will often modestly claim, when asked, that they are not great readers and certainly do not consider themselves writers. But we know this is untrue. They consume an astonishing amount of digital text and produce an equally astonishing amount. Although popular platforms like Instagram and Snapchat are image based, most students still necessarily swim in a sea of words. After all, even these platforms make use of descriptive text, and "texting" itself is ubiquitous. You must constantly decipher both images and words in order to navigate real-life social relationships and politics. After all, it takes work both to organize your weekend plans via text message and to sort out Blair's ilk from more reliable content providers.

> Students will often claim that they are neither great readers nor writers. But we know this is untrue. They consume an astonishing amount of digital text and produce an equally astonishing amount.

Many American undergraduate students have never known a world without constant internet access. And they have also never known a world without the so-called War on Terror and the conflicts that grew out of it. I vividly recall the events of 9/11 shattering my rather naïve view of a peaceful and ordered world. Perhaps the COVID-19 pandemic functioned much the same for you. Those of us born well prior to the events of both 9/11 and the novel coronavirus pandemic may remember a seemingly stable world order presided over by the benevolent presence of American democracy. I rather doubt many of you see the world through this lens today. Not surprisingly, the way in which the United States responded to the events of 9/11 and subsequent events deeply divided both Americans and others around the world. Around two decades later, our elected leaders and citizens alike are still arguing over the extent to which Americans should remain involved in military activity in Afghanistan – activity that began as a direct result of the 2001 terrorist attacks by Al Qaeda. Further debate continues over the extent to which the United States should engage newer terrorist groups like the Islamic State in Iraq and Syria (ISIS) around the world.

At the same time that Americans were increasingly fragmenting over questions of foreign and national security policy, the LGBTQ+ and other progressive movements quickly gathered momentum. As a result, for example, same-sex marriage went from a seemingly odd idea opposed by most prior to the twentieth-first century to a guaranteed constitutional right in 2015 after the landmark Supreme Court decision in *Obergefell v. Hodges*. The sheer speed of these changes exacerbated preexisting cultural divisions. Finally, during the presidencies of Barack Obama and Donald Trump, issues of structural racism and sexism in American society increasingly came to the forefront of the public imagination and left Americans more divided, and angry, than ever. I suspect that for many of my students, who cannot imagine a time prior to the traumas of the War on Terror, partisan rancor is simply a way of life.

As a result, for the past few years, my fellow professors and I have jokingly talked about living in "Weimar America," in reference to the politically polarized era of German history just prior to Hitler's ascent to power. Political division in America in general and on campuses in particular seems to be at an all-time high. Radical fringe elements on both the left and right are dominating the conversation. This is true in both my own classroom experience and that of colleagues. As a result, professors and students alike are debating the boundaries, if any, of free speech.[5] Does free speech mean the absence of all restrictions on speech? Or does it mean the ability to speak in promotion of the common good of diversity and inclusion? The rise of so-called fake news shared on social media and elsewhere further complicates matters. In this book, I'm defining "fake news" as news reporting that intentionally lies for financial or political gain. This fake news often feeds what some consider hate speech. Problematically, then, recent studies show that even college students are ill equipped to assess competing claims in the media.[6] Heated arguments based on either false or misleading content often give rise to bad argumentation. The internet, the classroom, and the dinner table are rife with fallacies that prevent clear thinking and compromise. And of course, the longer discussion continues, the closer everyone gets to finding more Hitlers.

In a time of political polarization, fake news, and frequently falla-cious argumentation, how can we know and convey the truth in an appealing manner? *Falsehood and Fallacy* addresses how students can evaluate what they read in a digital age, now that old institutional gate-keepers such as the press or institutions of higher education no longer hold a monopoly on disseminating knowledge. Short chapters cover current problems that derive from this flood of unmediated informa-tion, fake news, and bad arguments. Perhaps more importantly, though, we will work through how *you* can evaluate sources – including, and especially, online sources – critically.

In a time of political polarization, fake news, and frequently fal-lacious argumentation, how can we know and convey the truth in an appealing manner? *Falsehood and Fallacy* addresses how you can evaluate what you read in a digital age, now that old institutional gatekeepers such as the press or institutions of higher education no longer hold a monopoly on disseminating knowledge.

When was the last time you walked into a library and read phys-ical books or academic journals? Be honest. The temptation to sit in your pajamas on your bed and Google a research topic is simply too great. Obviously, I would be lying if I said I haven't done the same thing on occasion. According to a 2013 Pew Research Center study of American Advanced Placement (AP) and National Writing Proj-ect high school teachers, those surveyed believed that 94 per cent of students were "very likely" to use Google for research, 75 per cent were likely to use Wikipedia, and 52 per cent were likely to use YouTube. How many students used books that were not textbooks? Only 12 per cent.[7] Of course, the source material and its availability on the internet has been a great boon for researchers and the dissem-ination of knowledge in general. However, as a host of researchers have shown, even very bright college students often lack the skills to discern information that is relevant to their topic or even objectively true. To make matters worse, following the Great Recession of 2008, colleges and universities have been eliminating the types of program-ming that excel at teaching critical thinking and communications skills in favor of more narrowly career-oriented programming. The perception of many politicians and parents has been that in economically precarious times students cannot afford to "waste time" with studies that typically do not correspond directly to job opportunities. Historically, this perception has not been the reality. The mission of American colleges and universities has been to teach students the content and skills necessary to function as employed, active, and socially responsible citizens via a broad-based liberal education. The Association of American Colleges and Universities (AAC&U) defines a "liberal education" as an

> approach ... [that] emphasizes broad knowledge of the wider world (e.g., science, culture, and society) as well as in-depth achievement in a specific field of interest. It helps students develop a sense of social responsibility; strong intellectual and practical skills that span all major fields of study, such as communication, analytical, and problem-solving skills; and the demonstrated ability to apply knowledge and skills in real-world settings.[8]

Moreover, the AAC&U argues that in the twenty-first century, a liberal education has gone from being a nonvocational "option for the fortunate" to "essential for all students" because it is "essential for success in a global economy and for informed citizenship."[9] I agree with the AAC&U. More than ever, we cannot afford to limit the benefits of a liberal education to the privileged few.

Most colleges and universities offer students a liberal arts–based general education program during the first year or two of their studies. Then, later years are usually devoted to coursework in specific majors with learning outcomes that build on skills developed as part of the general education curriculum. While colleges must support undoubtedly important career-oriented majors or programs, like business or engineering, liberal arts disciplines like the humanities, sciences, and social sciences are no less vital. These liberal arts disciplines are important regardless of a student's major in part because they typically teach the basic skills needed not only to achieve vocational success but also to discern falsehoods and fallacies in the "real world." In other words, they teach students to critically assess sources and the content or claims of those sources. In practice, students tend to receive training in information literacy in first-year rhetoric and composition classes.[10] In theory, upper-level liberal arts classes build on and reinforce these skills. Sadly, in an attempt to attract more students and therefore more tuition revenue, some colleges and universities have begun trimming traditional liberal arts departments that could have collaborated with vocational programs to do just this. Perhaps most prominently, in 2018 the University of Wisconsin at Stevens Point announced it would eliminate thirteen majors including English, history, political science, and sociology.[11]

Defenders of the liberal arts and their role in a larger liberal education are surely right to note their very real economic value. Recent studies have shown that, far from inevitably winding up as bitter and underemployed baristas ten years after graduation, students who major in liberal arts disciplines generally do not earn substantially less than those in career-oriented majors and are often more satisfied in their careers.[12] More important, though, is the role of the liberal arts in educating for democracy regardless of which major students ultimately select. As Lynn Pasquerella, the president of the AAC&U, put it, "higher education is inextricably linked to our nation's historic mission of educating for democracy, [and] the work seems more urgent than ever" as a result of living in "an ostensibly post-truth era."[13] This is because without skills like informal logic and what historian Nigel Raab calls "critical exploration," the ability to discern truth from falsehood becomes impossible and democratic institutions necessarily suffer.[14]

Chapter Outline

This may all sound rather depressing. But don't despair. The book in your hands aims to help you read and research more critically so that you can make your own well-reasoned arguments, something desperately needed in our politically divided social landscape. However, before we can think critically or make our own arguments, we need to recognize first that we don't know everything. Indeed, even your professors, including me, do not know everything. We need to come at information and arguments with an open mind. Of course, an open mind does *not* mean an uncritical mind. Therefore, in chapter 2, we'll take a look at how the explosion of information and texts available on the internet has led to a proliferation of fake news and other falsehoods. The first part of this book, then, addresses the problem of falsehoods. We need to cultivate open critical minds now more than ever. This means realizing we don't know it all and therefore need to acquire the skills necessary to critically assess information.

In order to do this, we'll devote two chapters (3 and 4) to exploring some tools to help you evaluate sources and determine their legitimacy. Here I should note that I am a professional historian. As a result, I think and write like a historian. But, although the way I think about sources and their reliability is influenced by my own academic training, the basic skills I'll be discussing are applicable across a variety of different fields. Even if you are a business or biology major, this book is still for you. After all, all people need to be able to determine the credibility of what they read and hear on a daily basis. Next, in chapter 5, we'll talk about how to read sources critically. Even if a source is credible, you should still approach it with an analytical mind. You may think of reading as something you learn in grade school and then never need to reconsider. But this is simply not true. Just as an athlete needs constant practice and must continually seek out strategies for improvement, so too must good readers keep honing their craft over the course of a lifetime. Your college experience, and hopefully this book, will give you the skills and set you on the path to do just this.

Additionally, even if you determine a source is reliable in itself (and especially if it isn't), part of good reading involves constant vigilance for bad arguments and logical fallacies. Why talk about fallacies now? Political polarization tends to bring emotion to the surface and push logic to the back burner. As a result, fallacies flourish. Fallacies aren't necessarily errors in and of themselves. Rather, as historical logician David Hackett Fischer puts it, they are ways "of falling into error."[15] In general, a fallacious argument is an argument presented as though the conclusion is necessary – that we are compelled to accept it – when in fact, logically speaking, it is not the case. We need to be on guard against fallacies because a legitimate source can still contain false or misleading claims.[16] To contribute to this endeavor, the next three chapters (6, 7, and 8) in Part II will examine some of the formal and informal fallacies you are most likely to encounter and provide practice in recognizing them. This will help you learn how to read print and digital sources critically for understanding so that you can avoid being duped by the fallacies already discussed.

Falsehood and Fallacy concludes in a third part (chapter 9) by showing how reading like a skeptic and evaluating sources like a critic enables you to produce more clear and convincing academic writing. In fact, the idea and some of the content for this book came from my now defunct blog, *History Writing Demystified for the Undergraduate Scholar.* This chapter in particular pulls from that old 2016 blog and focuses on pitfalls or obstacles to clear in producing well-argued writing as opposed to the idea of "good" or "bad" writing. I embrace the idea that everyone is a writer and has aptitude for further growth. Moreover, because everyone is a writer, every career involves writing or communication in some capacity. Therefore, training as a writer is useful for you, because *you* are a writer. This is a philosophy I've adopted in theory as a result of working with writing center consultants, and it's also one I've learned in practice as a teacher. I have never known a student who was not also a writer. Ideally, this book will support student writers as you develop your own skills by providing a road map of obstacles to avoid along the way. As such, my methodology is not so much to teach students how to write, or to teach the process, as it is to illustrate hazards to avoid. In all, I hope this book and the short exercises included therein empower you to not be swept away by a flood of sometimes false or misleading information. Rather, chart your own course toward the truth and swim against fallacious currents as needed.

PART I

FALSEHOODS

CHAPTER 2

YOU'RE IN COLLEGE, BUT YOU DON'T KNOW EVERYTHING

Congratulations! If you're reading this chapter, you're probably in college. This means you've graduated from high school, successfully completed the relevant application forms, and been admitted. Well done. You may have a very specific career goal in mind at this point. Perhaps you're pre-med or you're planning on majoring in business or education. Maybe, like I did, you've been planning on majoring in history since high school. Or maybe you're undecided. I should note that "undecided" is one of the most popular majors among the students whom I advise. In many cases, undecided is also wise since it allows you to be open to a variety of potential majors or careers. In any case, when you think of "stuff you learn in college," you probably imagine high-level mathematics or literary theory. You may not immediately think of reading, research, critical analysis, and writing. Employers obviously value these skills immensely, as is evidenced by a veritable avalanche of popular articles and academic studies.[1] For example, a 2009 National Association of Colleges and Employers survey found that half of employers believed job candidates were unable to speak or write effectively.[2] This is especially problematic given that the same employers have consistently ranked the ability to communicate clearly as the most important quality in an employee.[3] In fact, developing desirable communication and other so-called soft skills are among the most important achievements of college graduates. Therefore, writing and communicating well isn't just for English majors; it's for everyone.

But the acquisition of job-related skills isn't the only, or even the primary, reason to attend college. Perhaps the Great Recession of

2008 caused educators to reemphasize the economic value of skills like critical thinking and writing. In any case, living as responsible and engaged citizens in a modern democracy also requires these skills. As a result, now is also the time to double down on their civic value. Thinking and communicating well don't just make students more employable. They make them better citizens. As Joan W. Scott, professor emerita at the Institute for Advanced Study in Princeton, said in a recent interview with Bill Moyers, the university is "supposed to teach citizens how to think better, how to think critically, how to tell the truth from falsehood, how to make a judgment about when they're being lied to and duped and when they're not, [and] how to evaluate scientific teaching."[4] Learning to distinguish truth from falsehood in order to serve the common good remains at the core of colleges' missions.

Now, more than ever, college instructors need to spend additional time helping students develop these abilities. I can still remember using the physical card catalog to find books in my hometown public library. The musty scent that emerged when you pulled open one of the Lilliputian drawers was enchanting and somehow simultaneously both soothing and exhilarating. The only books available were physical books, carefully shelved and maintained by dedicated professional librarians. Magazines were made of glossy paper and kept in their own special section of the library. I used to enjoy *Cat Fancy*, which featured glossy centerfolds of especially attractive purebred felines. If I needed to learn basic facts about something, I couldn't turn to Wikipedia or another online encyclopedia. The library kept actual encyclopedia collections. My family even bought me a World Book Encyclopedia collection from a real-live human traveling salesperson when I was in junior high school. Even in college and graduate school, when using a computer-based card catalog had become the norm and internet research was becoming more common, I still did most of my research using actual books and academic journals in libraries since I was set in my now antiquated ways. I even used a contraption called a microfilm reader to access copies of Victorian periodicals while in graduate school. If I set the microfilm reader before you today, many of you would quite possibly respond with the same look of bafflement my young daughter once directed toward a cassette tape player.

Technology and You

Of course, the invention and spread of access to the internet and now social media has changed everything. Today knowledge, opinions, and interpretation are endlessly available to us. Anyone with internet access can also access information on virtually any topic for free almost instantaneously from any location. Never has so much been available to so many for so little. Naturally, when I was a student in the 1990s, we trudged uphill to the library in waist-deep snow both ways. Today you lounge in the temperature-controlled comfort of your dorm room and Google "Kennedy assassination" or whatever your research paper topic happens to be. The moral of these stories is usually that the storyteller's generation had it so hard and your generation has it so easy. In fact, you probably do believe you have it easy thanks to the wonders of Google. I actually disagree. Instead, I would like to propose a counterintuitive interpretation of the impact of the internet on our ability to read, research, think, and write. Rather than make any of these things easier, it has actually made them *more* difficult.

I would like to propose a counterintuitive interpretation of the impact of the internet on our ability to read, research, think, and write. Rather than make any of these things easier, it has actually made them *more* difficult.

Communications critic Neil Postman begins his book *Technopoly* by recounting Plato's version of the story of the Egyptian pharaoh Thamus. In the myth, the god Theuth brought his inventions to Thamus for his approval. One of these inventions was writing, which Theuth described as "a sure receipt for memory and wisdom." Thamus, however, disagreed and argued that the unintended consequence of introducing writing to the Egyptian people would be the decay of their memories: "Those who acquire it [writing] will cease to exercise their memory and become forgetful; they will rely on writing to bring things to their remembrance by external signs instead of by their own internal resources." The moral Postman derives from this tale is that "it is a mistake to suppose that any technological innovation has a one-sided effect. Every technology is both a burden and a blessing; not either-or, but this-and-that."[5]

This has certainly been true of the introduction of the internet in ways few could have predicted when *Technopoly* was first published in 1992. Obviously, the internet and other forms of connectivity open up amazing new prospects for research. For example, whereas previously only a handful of researchers were able to access the original manuscripts of Walt Whitman's poems, these are now available online for anyone to examine for free at any time, thanks to the Walt Whitman Archive (https://whitmanarchive.org/). You can click on the link "In Whitman's Hand" to find enlargeable scanned images of the actual manuscript drafts of Whitman's poems and other works. If you took the time to put this book down and examine a few poem manuscripts, you know the Whitman Archive site is well maintained, is easy to use, and provides high-quality access to digital images. But how do you know that what you saw is real or trustworthy? How do you know that you were really looking at scanned images of the actual marks made by Whitman's hand? We'll come back to this problem later, but for now, let's just say that given the existence of so many websites with so many sources on the internet, it's increasingly challenging to determine what we can trust and what we can't.

In the era before "Theuth" metaphorically unleashed the internet, institutional gatekeepers such as schools, universities, libraries, academic publishers, newspapers of record, and network news outlets functioned as information filters. These organizations aimed to filter the factual and logical impurities out of our information stream in the way a filter on your faucet removes impurities from your water supply. Due to the inevitable existence of bias, the gatekeepers did occasionally filter out some important truths, and hence the importance of independent investigative journalism. At other times some bad interpretations slipped in, and hence the need for revisionist scholarship. However, by and large, schools, media institutions, and other gatekeepers ensured that most Americans consumed true information and cogent arguments.

This is no longer the case. The internet has essentially removed the filter from our drinking water. As a result, we receive our information from numerous sources, many of which are not reputable. You will find yourself swimming in a sea of unintentionally false misinformation, intentionally false disinformation, convincing satire, falsehoods, and fallacies. In the past, we did not constantly need to put as much effort into determining if a fact presented in a news story was true because the most accessible sources could usually be assumed reputable. But we now need to interrogate sources more carefully. What type of source is it? Regardless of the legitimacy of the source itself, does it provide accurate information and fallacy-free arguments? Given the speed at which content creators upload, revise, and remove sources, is an article I read yesterday even the same thing today and will it still be there tomorrow? Moreover, the internet has made the sheer number of sources available on any given topic increase exponentially. As a result, we are overwhelmed by source material. How can we know which sources to use and which to avoid?

Fake News

The problems associated with evaluating online sources have recently become all the more vexing because of the rise of "fake news." A 2019 Pew Research Center survey informs us that fully 50 per cent of Americans believe fake news is a "very big problem." To put this in perspective, fake news was seen as a big problem by more people than violent crime, climate change, racism, illegal immigration, terrorism, or sexism.[6] We can define "fake news" as reporting that is intentionally inaccurate, often for the sake of profit. It has obviously been around since the days of yellow, or exaggerated, journalism and even before. In the twenty-first century, however, websites and social media have allowed both misinformation and deliberate disinformation to spread more rapidly than ever, creating a new panic over the potential impact of false news reporting.

The reach of social media is many times greater than that of traditional print or television media. For example, ABC's and CBS's evening news shows each reach around nine million viewers. Facebook, on the other hand, reached 1.2 *billion* users per day in 2016.[7] Moreover, an increasingly large number of Americans use social media platforms as a primary source of news information. Prior to the advent of Facebook, most internet users searched Google for news content. By 2015, however, some researchers began to argue that more internet users had begun receiving their news via sharing than through direct Google searches.[8] A 2018 Pew Research Center study revealed that 68 per cent of American adults get news from social media, an increase of 6 per cent from 2016.[9] As of 2018, Facebook remained the major platform for sharing news stories, although the percentage of users who get news from Twitter, Reddit, YouTube, and Snapchat was growing.[10] Additionally, in 2018, for the first time, the percentage of Americans who reported often receiving their news from social media (20 per cent) was significantly higher than those who relied on print newspaper sources (16 per cent).[11]

Meanwhile, social media in its many different incarnations has become a launching pad for fake news. BuzzFeed media editor Craig Silverman publicly coined the term "fake news" in 2014 while he was studying the spread of misinformation as a fellow at Columbia University's Tow Center for Digital Journalism.[12] Since 2014, and especially since President Trump took office in 2017, politicians and partisan commentators have politicized the term. I, like Silverman, am using the term to refer to news content that contains deliberate lies for the purpose of profit or political persuasion.[13] Again, like Silverman, I am *not* referring to accidental errors made by journalists or editors nor to unconscious bias, although those are also factors of which readers should be aware. Silverman's initial work on fake news, which dealt with topics like the Ebola virus, garnered little attention until the 2016 US presidential election. At that point, the sheer volume of fake news – in the sense of deliberately false, partisan news stories designed to deceive readers – increased dramatically. This occurred in part owing to the partisan excitement generated by Trump's candidacy and the general rancor of the campaign.[14] The presence of a brash "outsider" candidate inflamed emotions, hardened echo chamber walls, and made partisans on both sides more likely to pass on "news" uncritically. Even after the election, "fake news" remained a constant presence on the internet and a source of consternation for many. In fact, by 2018, as a result of the fake news epidemic, 57 per cent of Americans simply assumed the news they consumed on social media was "largely inaccurate."[15]

Where does this fake news come from? And why produce it in the first place? Although fake news stories could be produced almost literally anywhere, Silverman discovered that one hotspot was the small city of Veles in Macedonia. Young adults in the Balkans – and elsewhere, for that matter – began creating websites to make a profit. Internet users would visit one of these websites and then click on the ads hosted by the site. This ad hosting enabled the website developers, who often lived in areas with few other viable economic opportunities, to make money. Meanwhile, the hyperpartisan 2016 US presidential election encouraged Americans to develop fake news websites either as intentional hoaxes or as satire. Many of the Macedonian websites had started out as apolitical, but Veles teenagers quickly discovered they could lift free political content from American satirical and hoax sites and pass it off as accurate news. The result was a rapid influx of site visitors and profit. In fact, some of the first Veles developers quickly began making up to $3,000 a day.[16]

Silverman notes that the amount of fake news shared on Facebook reached its peak in August 2016 after computer algorithms replaced the human journalists who had previously compiled lists of "trending" news.[17] Facebook argued that taking the compilation of trending news – a feature introduced in 2014 and eliminated in 2018 – out of human hands would reduce the possibility of political bias. However, without human fact-checkers to curb the algorithm's apparent mania for exotic partisan headlines, the algorithm spread both true and false stories with equal abandon. Trending topics included conservative commentator Megyn Kelly being removed from Fox News for supporting Democratic candidate Hillary Clinton and *Saturday Night Live* comedian Pete Davidson calling conservative writer Ann Coulter a "racist c★★★."[18] Problematically, in addition to letting accurate material of questionable journalistic value – like the Coulter story – spread like wildfire via the trending feature, the algorithm also spread false stories like the one about Kelly. Not surprisingly, then, when Silverman examined the top twenty fake news stories about the 2016 election and compared them with the top twenty election stories from nineteen legitimate news media sources, he found that "the fake news ones got more engagement on Facebook" between August and November.[19]

Bubbles and Echo Chambers

Some of these fake news stories were convincing, others less so. Nevertheless, even not-very-convincing stories – about Pope Francis endorsing Trump for president, for example, and about an FBI agent associated with Clinton dying in a murder-suicide – spread like wildfire around social media platforms. Stories like these seem plausible to us because of what leftist internet activist Eli Pariser calls the "filter bubble."[20] More than ever before, we have become disconnected from real-life communities made up of people with a variety of political and religious views. Instead, we curate groups of like-minded friends on Instagram, Snapchat, Facebook, and other social media sites. Is someone angering you with their political blathering? Do you just flat-out disagree? You can unfriend or block her. In real life you may try, but this is considerably less easy to do – especially if this person is your roommate or cousin.

The result of this loss of intellectual diversity is an inability to empathize with those who disagree with you. They must be wrong, because everyone you know agrees with you. Pariser talks about this as living in a bubble that filters out all dissonant ideas. Unfortunately, these ideologically filtered groups can quickly degenerate into mobs that attack "impure" outsiders. In these situations, disagreeing with the group majority could cause you to be cast out of the group into the outer darkness where there is weeping and gnashing of teeth. Here we should point out that spending too much time in a filtered bubble can cause you to fall prey to the *bandwagon fallacy*, an informal fallacy we will discuss in greater detail in a later chapter. In this fallacy, it appears that something must be true because everybody thinks it is. However, objective truth is not determined by how many people – even if they are your friends – believe it or not.

In any case, ideological echo chambers also intensify confirmation bias. The term "confirmation bias" refers to the phenomenon that people are more likely to believe information that supports their existing beliefs. After all, nobody wants to be wrong. The types of filtered bubbles we find on Facebook and other social media platforms more firmly entrench our beliefs and therefore render confirmation bias even more likely. Confirmation bias is an essential component to the spread of fake news. Without it, we would be less likely to believe and share stories about President Trump ordering the execution of the Thanksgiving turkeys that President Obama had once pardoned.[21] In another setting, you might have a Trump-supporting friend who would ask you to be more critical of this story. Unfortunately, this type of critical evaluation is increasingly unlikely to happen in filtered online communities.

Interestingly, not all social media sites create bubbles. Twitter – currently Facebook's biggest competitor in terms of reach – generally allows *everyone* on the platform to see all posts. Unless you change the settings, only those you've identified as friends see your posts on Facebook timelines. If you are posting in a group, the number of potential views is even smaller and probably also even less ideologically diverse. Twitter, however, automatically allows all 320 million-plus users to see your tweet. The result, as James Ball notes in his book *Post-Truth: How Bullshit Conquered the World*, is to incite angry mob-like behavior between ideological adversaries.[22] Ironically, the impact of Twitter mob behavior is similar to the echo chamber that results from Facebook's curated communities. Those caught up in the resulting tweet-storm become less likely to break from the group dynamic, more radicalized in their opinions, more likely to fall prey to confirmation bias, and therefore less likely to be critical thinkers and more likely to believe and retweet fake news.

The Spread of Fake News

As a result of all this, the prevalence and influence of ideological bubbles and especially fake news itself became one of the biggest stories of the 2016 election.[23] Scientists released a veritable flood of studies – many of which had begun considerably prior to the election campaign – to explore the interactions between social media and fake news. For example, thanks to a major new study of three million Twitter users led by MIT data scientist Soroush Vosoughi, we now know that fake news presented as clickbait (content designed primarily to attract viewers) spreads considerably more quickly and reaches more people than true news stories. In fact, fake news reaches 1,500 people on Twitter an average of six times more quickly than true news.[24] Additionally, this fake news was 70 per cent more likely to be retweeted than true news. While true news stories were generally only able to form chains of ten retweets, fake news could form chains of nineteen retweets ten times as fast as it took the true news to form the smaller chains. Vosoughi concludes that "it seems to be pretty clear [from our study] that false information outperforms true information."[25] And fake news continues to spread like a giant fungus despite efforts to educate the public about the problem. Silverman concluded that the fifty biggest fake news stories of 2017 generated even more visits than the top fifty fake news stories of 2016.[26]

As for why it spreads so quickly, Vosoughi hypothesizes that fake news is more exciting because it is "novel." Of course, to believe that fake news (or anything else) is true because of its novelty or surprise factor is to fall prey to the *appeal to novelty fallacy*, an informal logical fallacy. The fact that something is novel has no bearing on its truth value, or on whether or not we should retweet it. The MIT researchers also argued that fake news spread more quickly because clickbait titles and content evoke more emotion than true news.[27] Simply put, outrage generates shares, which generate clicks, which generate money for the creators of fake news stories. Political scientist Rebekah Tromble argues that "the key takeaway is really that content that *arouses strong emotions* spreads further, faster, more deeply, and more broadly on Twitter."[28] One recent example of this phenomenon may be the Momo hoax of early 2019. A story about a children's challenge game featuring a hideous character called Momo exploded onto social media. News outlets quickly noticed the story and warned parents against the game, in which Momo supposedly urged players to injure or kill themselves. As it turns out, the whole Momo challenge was a hoax, yet the story rapidly went viral – largely owing to the emotional shock of children potentially killing themselves in response to a game and Momo's ugly visage itself.[29] Again, just because a news story or argument appeals to your emotions, you should not necessarily believe it. The *appeal to emotion* is yet another informal logical fallacy that we will explore in more detail in a later chapter.

Not only do fake news stories spread untrue information across social media very, very quickly, but they also make it harder for legitimate journalists and news outlets to cover the news. The sense that seemingly any fact one encounters on the internet could potentially be untrue allows readers to label accurate news stories with inconvenient facts as fake news. Moreover, since President Trump labeled CNN as a purveyor of fake news, on January 11, 2017, the term has become a political weapon.[30] Media outlets once seen as authoritative now find themselves labeled as purveyors of fake news on the same level as Alex Jones's InfoWars, a website notorious for spreading right-wing conspiracy theories. In such an environment, does the actual source of the news story even matter? Perhaps not for many. Such a conclusion may be borne out by another recent study of online news consumption, performed by the Pew Research Center. According to Pew, only 56 per cent of respondents could provide the name of a news source they had visited within the past two hours.[31] Interestingly, young adults (eighteen to twenty-nine years old) were *more* likely to forget the news source than older respondents (57 per cent for adults aged thirty to forty-nine and 61 per cent for those fifty and older).[32] In any case, the resulting relativism regarding the news has given rise to "post-truth politics." In other words, we now live in an era in which the actual truth of a claim seems irrelevant to its political import.

Discerning Truth and Falsehood

When it comes to online activity, older researchers have long assumed that Millennials, and especially post-Millennials, are digital natives who have no difficulties discerning truth from falsehood on the internet. Yes, the interest is awash with conflicting versions of events and truth claims, but academics often assume that young people raised on the internet are more capable of discerning legitimate from illegitimate sources and truth from falsehood than older generations. Clearly, they should have been able to determine that the widely shared 2016 "Pizzagate" news story connecting presidential candidate Hillary Clinton, child sex trafficking, and a pizzeria was untrue.

We now know that this assumption was wishful thinking. In 2015 historian Sam Wineburg and his colleagues at the Stanford History Education Group (SHEG) began formally assessing the ability of seven thousand middle-school students, high school students, and university students to critically evaluate what they read online. The results of the study – released on November 22, 2016, shortly after the presidential election – were not encouraging. As Wineburg put it in the executive summary, "Overall, young people's ability to reason about the information on the Internet can be summed up in one word: *bleak*."[33] Bleak may be an appropriate word here: youth had difficulty critically evaluating both the sources themselves and the claims made in the sources.

The Stanford researchers designed a series of exercises to determine the extent to which students could assess the trustworthiness of internet sources. Test subjects at each grade level participated in five different exercises. The report's executive summary highlights three, including analyzing a home page, for middle-school students; determining the trustworthiness of a photograph shared on Imgur, for high school students; and determining the ways in which a tweet might or might not prove to be a useful source of information, for university students.[34] Wineburg found the results disappointing, to say the least. For example, over 80 per cent of middle-school students didn't realize that sponsored-content articles were in fact advertisements and not real news stories.[35] High school students examined an arresting photograph of supposedly mutated flowers. The image was accompanied by text indicating that the flowers' "mutations" were caused by the Fukushima nuclear disaster in Japan. The research group found that fewer than 20 per cent of the respondents questioned the source of the photograph.[36] The findings for college students were not much more promising. Students struggled to analyze a tweet from the liberal activist group MoveOn.org regarding gun control. They were shown an image of the tweet, including its blue and white verification badge illustrating its authenticity. Yet, relatively few students noted that the survey results referenced in the tweet, which originated with a professional polling organization, Public Policy Polling, could be "useful" in research. Additionally, few noted that the liberal orientation of MoveOn.org may have influenced how the poll was constructed and used.[37]

In short, the SHEG study confirms the findings of earlier studies that children and young adults tend to consume media content without distinguishing among the legitimacy of sources or evaluating the accuracy of the content itself.[38] The results of the study are especially significant since, according to the Media Insight Project, 88 per cent of adults between the ages of eighteen and thirty-four regularly consume news from Facebook and other social media platforms.[39] If we lived under a different form of government – one not dependent on citizen participation – we could perhaps ignore these findings. However, as Wineburg notes, "democracy is threatened by the ease at which disinformation about civic issues is allowed to spread and flourish."[40]

How can young people, or anyone for that matter, make informed decisions about the future of their countries when they are unable to sift out truths from untruths? Moreover, since commentators slap the "fake news" label *both* on sources spreading intentional misinformation *and* on media sources that attempt to provide accurate news (despite mistakes and biases), we all need to be able to evaluate sources. Part of the solution is to develop the reading, critical evaluation, and writing skills associated with the practice of history and related disciplines. In a 2016 article, Wineburg notes that it is one thing for a young adult to be a "digital native and quite another to be digitally *intelligent*."[41] My minor quibble with Professor Wineburg here is that I do think digital natives are, in fact, also digitally intelligent. I think the real problem is that most people of all ages simply haven't had the opportunity to develop all the skills necessary to discern the true from the false. As a result, well-meaning citizens fall prey to both fake news and, not infrequently, bad arguments. This is not surprising. After all, we don't know it all. As a college student you are lucky to have the chance to hone the skills needed to learn new information and realize what you do and don't know. The remainder of this book, therefore, provides you with a toolbox of the skills you'll need to think critically, discern the truth, and become an informed citizen in a post-truth world. Like Wineburg, I say "historical skills" not because I'm seeking to turn you into a professional historian (not that that would be a bad thing) but because the skills historians use to interrogate arguments and sources are precisely the skills needed by *everyone*.[42]

Website Content Exercise

In September 2020 I took three screenshots from the website of the Post Millennial (https://thepostmillennial.com/), a Canadian online "news, politics, culture, and lifestyle" magazine. Can you determine which screenshots contain news stories and opinion pieces? Which contain advertisements? How do you know?

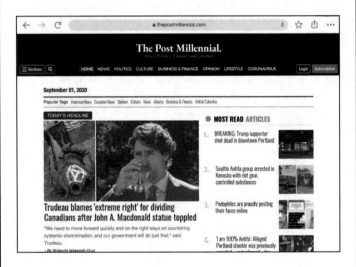

Answer

The first image contains political news stories. The second image contains an advertisement. The third image also contains an advertisement. You can tell which links go to advertisements on this site because they are set off from the main body of links. The offset box is labeled "Ad" in the upper left corner. Also, running your cursor over the arrow in the upper right-hand corner of the suspected advertisement would cause "AdChoices" to pop up. AdChoices is an advertising program that uses the websites you visit and your browsing history to determine the types of advertisements you will see. Sponsored-content "stories" are a less obvious form of advertising. These appear in online news magazines like Slate (https://slate.com/) and Vox (https://www.vox.com) and are explicitly labeled as "sponsored content." Other online news or opinion sites will explicitly state that certain links or stories are "promoted" by another site.

Tweet Authenticity Exercise

How can you tell this is an authentic tweet from President Donald Trump?[43]

Donald J. Trump ✔
@realDonaldTrump   ○○○

A very big part of the Anger we see today in our society is caused by the purposely false and inaccurate reporting of the Mainstream Media that I refer to as Fake News. It has gotten so bad and hateful that it is beyond description. Mainstream Media must clean up its act, FAST!

7:18 AM · Oct 25, 2018 · Twitter for iPhone

41K Retweets   **15.1K** Quote Tweets   **154.1K** Likes

Answer
The white check mark within the blue badge indicates that Twitter has verified that the user of the handle @realDonaldTrump is, in fact, President Donald J. Trump. Of course, a person could create an image that merely *looks* like an actual tweet with a verification badge but was never a genuine tweet. Therefore, if you see an image of a tweet on social media, especially if it is controversial, check the supposed user's Twitter feed to see if the tweet did in fact originate from that handle. For a major figure like Trump, you should also see if news outlets and fact-checkers have corroborated the authenticity of a given tweet. Given the sheer volume of tweets produced by Trump, and their importance, some individuals and organizations have also created online archives of the president's tweets. In this case, you could check Brendan Brown's Trump Twitter Archive or CNN's All the President's Tweets to see if your tweet has been archived as genuine.[44]

CHAPTER 3

EVALUATING STATEMENTS AND IDENTIFYING SOURCES

How to Dodge Falsehoods

Now that we've had an introduction to the problems associated with falsehoods, let's get on to the twin plagues of fakes and fallacies. If falsehood-bearing fake news is contaminating our social media diet, how can we know what is safe for consumption and what isn't? The next two chapters open up the historian's skill set, which is applicable beyond the discipline, and pull out some concepts and techniques to help you better evaluate sources and their content. The first part of this chapter will help you think about the types of statements and claims made within sources and how to differentiate among them. Broadly speaking, this chapter deals with the issue of objectivity vs. subjectivity in sources. If you don't know what those words mean, don't worry. We'll define them below. The second part of this chapter will help you differentiate between various types of sources. Also, please note that I'm absolutely not only talking about online sources here. I hope that in college – and for the rest of your lives – you'll be reading many print sources. Most of these concepts and skills are applicable to any type of source you may encounter, whether print or online.

The Merriam-Webster Dictionary defines something as objective if it exists apart from the mind. Something is subjective if it does not. So, the professor lecturing in front of you exists objectively; the boredom in your head is subjective.

Fact vs. Opinion

Before even considering whether a source or, more specifically, a statement in a source is true or not, you should determine what *kind* of statement it is. This is because you wouldn't want to waste your time trying to determine whether certain types of statements, like opinions, are true or false when, by definition, they are impossible to verify. An important distinction exists between factual statements and statements of opinion. According to the Pew Research Center, a "factual statement" is something that can be either proven or disproven based on objective evidence.[1] Something is objective if it exists separately from your mind. We could make a further distinction between factual statements and facts more narrowly. Facts are factual statements that are proven and therefore true. Ideally, everyone should agree with facts.[2]

Without diving into philosophical intricacies, an opinion, for our purposes, is a view based on beliefs arrived at in the absence of objective evidence.[3] Opinions are subjective, value-based beliefs that cannot be objectively proven or disproven. Again, things are objective if they exist independently of a person's consciousness and outside of the individual's own experience. In contrast, things are subjective if they only exist within your consciousness and within your own experience of them. It's important to keep in mind, though, that opinions could be true and factual statements could be false. So the distinction isn't in whether things are true or false but in whether they can possibly be *proven* to be true or false.

> **Factual statement:** a statement that can be either proven or disproven based on objective evidence
> **Fact:** a factual statement that is proven and therefore true
> **Opinion:** a subjective statement that cannot be either proven or disproven based on objective evidence

In order to ferret out fake news and other falsehoods, you should know which statements can be proven true and which cannot. It may surprise you that a recent Pew Center study of 5,035 American adults conducted between February 22 and March 8, 2018, revealed that a only a small percentage of the population can tell the difference.[4] The study asked participants to identify political statements as factual statements or opinions. Only 26 per cent correctly identified all five factual statements and only 35 per cent correctly identified all five opinion statements. The study's authors note that "this result is only a little better than random guesses."[5] The study also revealed that participants were more likely to mark a statement as factual when it supported their political biases. This should alert us to the problem of confirmation bias and how it colors our interpretation of sources.

One takeaway here is that we need to be aware of our own biases. Simply because you *want* something to be factual because it supports your position does not mean that it is. Moreover, participants "overwhelmingly" believed that statements that were factual were also *true*, or accurate.[6] However, this is not necessarily the case. Again, not all factual statements are true. Rather, factual statements are merely capable of being proven either true *or* false. This means that when reading a textual source, be it in print or online, you'll need to not only distinguish between opinion statements and factual statements but also determine the accuracy (truth) of the factual statements. That's two layers of evaluation. First, you'll need to determine if a statement is capable of being proven true based on objective evidence. Then you'll need to examine the evidence to see if it really is true or not. This isn't always easy, but read on for more tools to help you discern fact from opinion and truth from falsehood.

Exercises on Factual Statements vs. Opinion

Evaluate the following statements to determine if they are facts (true factual statements) or opinions.[7] Note: there may be some room to debate whether or not the following statements are entirely factual or entirely opinion.

1) The worst measles outbreak in the United States since 1994 occurred in 2019.
2) Too much government makes people less self-sufficient and damages their self-esteem.

3) An American interventionist foreign policy always makes the world a more dangerous place.
4) People who oppose childhood vaccinations don't have the best interests of humanity in mind.
5) The fantasy TV series *Game of Thrones* lasted for eight seasons.
6) Season eight of *Game of Thrones* was the worst season.
7) The "AR" in the AR-15 semiautomatic rifle stands for "ArmaLite Rifle," not assault rifle.
8) Pro-life activists are anti-woman.
9) Attending a four-year liberal arts college is necessary to be truly educated.
10) In December 2018, US defense secretary Jim Mattis resigned from his position.

Answers
1) Factual statement. We can measure the number of measles cases occurring in the United States each year, so this statement can be either proven or disproven.
2) Opinion. You could devise various quantitative (number-based) and qualitative ways to measure a person's self-sufficiency, but since the very concept of self-sufficiency is itself subjective, it is impossible to objectively determine whether or not "too much government" makes people less self-sufficient. Moreover, how much is too much? The whole idea of "too much" is itself subjective and therefore opinion based. One person's too much will be someone else's too little. Finally, it's impossible to objectively measure damage to someone's self-esteem, which is a subjective experience.
3) Opinion. This is also an opinion because while we could attempt to quantify the number of conflicts that occurred during interventionist American administrations, it is impossible to quantify the number that would have occurred were it not for those same interventionist administrations. Moreover, *interventionist* is subjective. What one person may consider interventionist, another may not. Even the concept of danger can be subjective.
4) Opinion. This is an opinion because people who do not vaccinate their children may very well sincerely believe that they have the best interests of humanity in mind. And,

again, people can disagree about what the best interests of humanity is. Some may think it is to prevent the spread of measles and other contagious diseases. Others may think it is to prevent the spread of disorders they believe are caused by vaccinations.

5) Factual statement. This is a factual statement because a quick check of HBO's *Game of Thrones* official website (https://www.hbo.com/game-of-thrones) reveals that the series did, in fact, last eight seasons.

6) Opinion. This is an opinion because it is based purely on subjective taste. Although I haven't met any yet, some people may have liked the eighth season of *Game of Thrones* more than the earlier seasons.

7) Factual statement. A little internet research will inform you that "AR" does indeed stand for "ArmaLite Rifle." See "Modern Sporting Rifle: Introduction," National Shooting Sports Foundation, accessed August 17, 2020, https://www.nssf.org/msr/; and Greg Myre, "A Brief History of the AR-15," February 28, 2018, NPR, https://www.npr.org/2018/02/28/588861820/a-brief-history-of-the-ar-15.

8) Opinion. Many pro-life activists argue that they are pro-women. Being "pro-" or "anti-" woman is subjective.

9) Opinion. This is an opinion because what "truly educated" means is subjective. Some would argue that training in a craft like welding makes one truly educated.

10) Factual statement. Research can easily show when Jim Mattis resigned.

Interpretation vs. Opinion

Related to the distinction between fact and opinion is the distinction between interpretation and opinion. Interpretations make sense of, or explain, facts. Have you ever debated a friend or enemy (or frenemy?) and at some point your exasperated opponent declared "Well, that's just your opinion!" in order to end the conversation? I know it's certainly happened to me. Calling a statement an "opinion" shuts off conversation because opinions are subjective and not subject to verification. Therefore, why should your opponent give your statement serious consideration? As a professor, I've seen the same thing occur in the classroom. A student may disagree with an author. I ask the student why he disagrees and he claims the author's interpretation of the event in question was "just his opinion." The rest of the class then nods in silent agreement. But is everything we read or discuss in the classroom just one person's subjective opinion? Are we forever trapped in relativism? In other words, is there no absolute truth that is not merely relative to individuals or cultures?

In response to this problem, we should first recall the distinction between factual and opinion statements discussed above. Obviously not all statements are opinions. Some are factual and we need to know the difference. But I'd like to also bring up the very important distinction between what we commonly call opinion and interpretation. Opinion, as historian Kevin Passmore defines it, is "speculation in the absence of knowledge." Oftentimes, though, what we call "opinion" is really an interpretation. An interpretation is an explanation that depends "on the supporting *evidence*, and on the citation ... of relevant facts."[8] Interpretations "are based on evidence and facts, which differentiates them from mere opinion."[9] Rather than just offer a factual statement, interpretations *explain* based on relevant objective evidence. Interpretations, then, unlike opinions, can be more or less probable based on their use of evidence. If an interpretation does not make sense of evidence or is not supported adequately by facts, it is not a strong interpretation. The best interpretation always provides the best *explanation*. Genuine opinions, on the other hand, have no explanatory power in and of themselves since they are statements that arise in the absence of factual evidence. The interpretation that makes the most sense of the relevant evidence is the most probable. If the evidence is flimsy, then an interpretation is bound to be highly improbable. Therefore, to weed out bad interpretations you'll need to determine just *how* probable a given interpretation is by examining the evidence, or sources, used to underpin the interpretation.

One way to think about the difference between interpretation and opinion is to imagine a jigsaw puzzle. Each of the pieces is a piece of evidence. An interpretation is a description of what the finished puzzle looks like based on having first examined the individual pieces. An opinion is a guess as to what the finished puzzle will look like, without first examining the pieces. Interpretations, then, are built on evidence and facts, unlike genuine opinions. So if your "opinion" is verifiable, it's not really an opinion at all.

The distinction between opinion and interpretation can be confusing, however, especially when it comes to the fraught task of writing research papers. For example, just a few months ago, I was sitting in my office and I accidentally overheard a conversation taking place in the hallway right outside my door. A student had caught another professor walking down the hall and engaged her in conversation about a rough draft of his research paper. When the professor suggested that the research paper should be argumentative in nature and contain sources to support his interpretations, the student asked if that meant putting in more opinions. The professor and student then retreated to an office, presumably for further discussion. The problem here was that the student failed to differentiate between fact-based interpretation or analysis and opinions. What the professor wanted was interpretation, which entails an explanation based on relevant evidence.

Interpretations are explanations based on evidence. Opinions are beliefs held in the absence of evidence.

Whether you are listening to the political pontifications of your roommate or reading a news story on climate change, try to distinguish between opinion and interpretation. If the arguer offers no evidence, then, although the arguer may turn out to be correct, you have no compelling reason to believe the claim. Feel free to turn off the TV or disregard the meme. If the arguer offers an interpretation based on evidence, however, you do have a solid reason to believe the claim and should investigate it further. This will involve evaluating the sources used to support the claim and assessing the accuracy of any factual statements. Again, though, note that while a researcher can objectively prove or disprove factual statements and thereby show them to be either true or false, an interpretation is only more or less probable because it is an explanation assembled from evidence.

Interpretation begins with the act of selecting facts or sources.

Some students also worry that the inevitable presence of bias in interpreters renders all interpretations equally subjective. After all, even if an author has tried as hard as possible to be objective, all interpretations remain biased in some sense. However, this does *not* mean that all interpretations are equally probable. The presence of bias does not make it impossible to discern which evidence an author has used or if the factual statements undergirding his interpretation are accurate.[10] Nevertheless, authors who are aware of the potential for bias and strive for maximal objectivity are more likely to offer strong interpretations of evidence than those who do not. For this reason, the best academic and journalistic writing always strives for objectivity, even if strict neutrality is impossible.

Exercise on Opinion vs. Interpretation

Determine if the conclusions below are opinions or interpretations based on *relevant* evidence. Then, ask why you answered the way you did. Some of these cases are more difficult than others and there could be some room for debate. If possible, you may want to discuss these initially in small groups.

1) People who are concerned about climate change are annoying. They just want to make life more difficult for everyone who can't afford a solar-powered car.

2) The largest number of public Confederate memorials were built during the Jim Crow era, following the *Plessy v. Ferguson* court case that legally established racial segregation in 1896.[11] These monuments may have originated at least partially as part of the effort to bolster segregation in American society.

3) Most of the people living in America with disease X traveled from a specific country. This country was probably the origin of disease X.

4) Meta-analysis shows that the measles, mumps, and rubella (MMR) vaccine is "not associated with the development of autism or autism spectrum disorder."[12] It's wrong to allow parents to opt out of vaccinating their children through "conscience clauses."

5) In April 2017 nearly one hundred people were killed in a chemical weapons attack in Syria.[13] Chemical weapons are the worst type of weapons.

Answers

1) Opinion: These statements are not directly supported by any evidence. Additionally, calling someone annoying is a subjective judgment.

2) Interpretation: This statement does marshal quantitative data in support of its conclusion.

3) Interpretation: Again, this statement uses data and inductive reasoning to support its conclusion.

4) Opinion: The conclusion about conscience clauses does not necessarily follow from the premise about the MMR vaccine not being associated with autism. In other words, the evidence given does not correspond or may be irrelevant to the religious and moral concerns of those seeking conscience exemptions and whether or not those exemptions should be allowed.

5) Opinion: The conclusion does not directly follow. Moreover, if we are using "worst" to mean the type of weapon that has killed the most people in the conflict in Syria, then more people have been killed in other ways. The author may want to define "worst" in another way, but the evidence provided is only relevant to quantification or the number of deaths.

Objectivity vs. Neutrality

You may wonder at this point why there is so much unpleasant disagreement about politics, economics, religion, and even some areas of the physical sciences. If interpretations are based on factual statements, and factual claims can be proven or disproven, then shouldn't we be able to investigate all factual statements and agree on the interpretation that best explains them? Although it would be simpler if this were the case, we do not discover true facts and then interpret them. Rather, interpretation begins with the act of selecting facts or sources. As historian John Arnold writes,

> The sources do not "speak for themselves" and never have done [so]....
> They come alive when the historian reanimates them. And although the
> sources are a beginning, the historian is present before or after, using
> skills and making choices. Why *this* document and not another? Why
> *these* charters and not those?[14]

Sources, in other words, need someone to select and interpret them.
Passmore writes that the historian E.H. Carr gave three reasons for
this: the number of sources, source unreliability, and the role of bias in
interrogating sources. First, there are too many sources and too many
factual statements about any given topic for any one person to interpret successfully. Therefore, when facing this embarrassment of riches,
the interpreter must select which sources he or she will interpret. But,
given the impossibility of shedding all bias, the determination of which
sources are the most relevant becomes itself "an act of interpretation."[15]
The second problem is that the sources from which researchers mine
evidence are messy. Any source could be unreliable in any number of
ways and will need to undergo critical evaluation. Finally, Passmore
adds to Carr's list that even if – hypothetically – interpreters had only
a single source with which to understand a topic, they would still need
to determine which question to ask about the source. Here again, bias
creeps in.

With these points in mind, is pure objectivity possible? Not according to Passmore, among many others.[16] Is everything really just an opinion after all? Opinions obviously make no claim to objectivity, since
they are subjective conjectures by definition. Interpretations, on the
other hand, can be more or less plausible depending on the veracity
of the evidence and the strength of the inferences drawn therefrom.
Of course, the fact that interpretations are always only more or less
plausible means that they can never be established with 100 per cent
certainty. Does this mean that everything is relative and all interpretations are equally valid?[17] Is all meaning only subjective? Do we live
in a post-truth world with objectivity relegated to the status of being
only a "noble dream"?[18] This isn't necessarily the case.

Historian Carl Trueman makes a helpful distinction between what
he calls "objectivity" and "neutrality" in his book *Histories and Fallacies*. He defines neutrality as freedom from bias and notes that whereas
neutrality is an unachievable ideal, objectivity, properly defined, is

not.[19] Despite much hand-wringing among professional historians over the possibility of objectivity in the past few decades, objectivity simply means being open to independent "verification" by anyone using testable "public criteria."[20] These procedures differ by discipline. The natural sciences, of course, use the famous scientific method. The empirical scientific method, first developed in the early modern period, begins by asking a question and performing the necessary research. The questioner then forms a hypothesis, which he or she tests through an experiment and then analyzes. Finally, the questioner writes up the results as a report.

> Trueman defines neutrality as being free from bias. This is impossible. He defines objectivity as openness to independent verification using publicly known criteria. In this sense, objectivity is possible.

Historians like Trueman use the historical method, which developed out of the scientific method. As history developed into a formal academic discipline in European universities, practitioners turned to the scientific method to make their craft as objective, and therefore legitimate, as possible. Although there is no one iteration of the historical method, it usually contains the following elements: a student asks a question and formulates a hypothesis. She then conducts research and evaluates sources capable of providing relevant evidence. At this point, she has either disproven the initial hypothesis or raised new questions. In either case, it's back to the library – or, more likely these days, to the internet. Once a student has enough evidence to prove her thesis, the student then writes out her findings in the form of an argumentative research paper.

The scientific and historical methods – and the methods used in other academic disciplines – are not secrets. Anyone can independently verify the conclusions reached and determine whether the interpretation adequately explains the data. When we think about the possibility of an academic paper, a news story, or a blog post being "objective," let's not think so much about whether or not it's wholly free from bias: it's not. No one can be purely neutral. Instead, let's take Trueman's suggestion and think about whether the interpretation of factual statements and other evidence in a source can be publicly verified or not.[21] These distinctions, including the one between objectivity and neutrality, are important because they help us distinguish between truths and falsehoods.

Types of Sources: Primary vs. Secondary Sources

So far we've talked about reading sources at a fairly theoretical level. Now it's time to get practical. First, one of the most important initial skills to have when encountering a source is the ability to say exactly what kind of source it is. This is because different types of sources may need to be evaluated in different ways. Evidence comes in two major types of sources: primary and secondary. Differentiating between primary and secondary sources helps us to evaluate a source in history and beyond.

> Primary sources give direct access to the thing under study. Secondary sources give indirect interpretations of the thing under study.

Primary sources are firsthand accounts of the thing you are studying. They provide evidence about these things, which could be virtually anything, such as a past or present event, person, or object. The important thing to remember about primary sources is that they originate in the period under study and give you direct access to whatever you are researching.[22] Texts such as government documents, newspaper and magazine stories reporting on contemporary events, census records, diary entries, letters, and autobiographies constitute primary sources. If you were studying the American Revolution, then the Declaration of Independence, written in 1776, would be an example of a primary source. As you undoubtedly know, though, not all texts exist as pen-and-ink manuscripts. These days, scholars also consider online newspaper stories, blog entries, emails, texts, and tweets as primary sources.

Furthermore, most sources are not text at all. If you stop to think about how you gather information about the world around you, you'll probably realize that only a fraction of it comes from reading text. We shouldn't forget works of art, cartoons, photographs, and increasingly internet memes, which combine both stock images and text. Additionally, consider audible sources, such as music or audio recordings of eyewitness testimony, for example. Material objects can also be primary sources. If you plan to go into a scientific field, you should know that your own experimental data, even if it is put into published charts and tables, is primary source material.

What are secondary sources, then? Secondary sources, unlike primary sources, make nonfiction secondhand interpretations of the things under study. These interpretations derive from primary sources and/or other secondary sources.[23] Again, these sources can take on a variety of forms, most obviously books and articles written about the subject under study. If you were still conducting research for that essay on the American Revolution, a history textbook or an academic book (a monograph) would be a secondary source. The monograph makes an argument about the Revolution based on primary sources like the Declaration of Independence. The resulting written narrative interpretation is a secondary source. Other types of secondary sources, besides books, include peer-reviewed academic articles, review essays, editorial or interpretative pieces published in magazines and newspapers, or analyses of experimental data obtained by others. Some also categorize contemporary news reports as secondary sources if the reporter is synthesizing direct accounts as opposed to providing her own.

This is the basic distinction between primary and secondary sources, but things can get a little tricky. Some sources can actually be *either* a primary source *or* a secondary source depending on the context. Here's one example I use in my world history class. Imagine that after you finished writing your research paper on the American Revolution you – for some unthinkable reason – threw your textbook into the trash can. The sadly discarded book, which was for you a secondary source, then traveled to the local landfill, only to be covered over with rubbish and soil and finally forgotten. But, behold, a hundred years later, a group of intrepid archeologists digging in the old landfill unearth your old textbook! This is wonderfully exciting for them, since the textbook has a copyright date of 2020 and the archeologists are part of an interdisciplinary group of scholars studying American historical perspectives in the year 2020! Now, would the textbook be a primary source for this group of academics or a secondary source? If you answered primary source, you would be correct. Why? Because the textbook was written and published in 2020 and provides a historical perspective written by an American. As a result, it reflects the craft practiced by an American historian in 2020.

We should also note that when it comes to supporting an argument, not all sources are created equal. Primary sources are the best or most authoritative types of evidence, followed by secondary sources. But even within the larger category of secondary sources, there is a hierarchy. At the top are academic sources. Academic sources have gone through a process known as peer review. Editors submit academic book manuscripts and journal articles to double-blind review by other experts in the relevant field. "Double-blind" here means that the author of the peer-reviewed source does not know who the reviewers are and the reviewers do not know who the author is. This method assures some level of neutrality on the part of the reviewers. The peer reviewers, or referees, give the author constructive criticism with the goal of improving the writing and ensuring it meets appropriate publication standards. This is not unlike the way your professors review and assess your own writing.

The next time your professor returns a piece of writing to you covered in comments, remember that he or she has had the same experience many times over as part of the peer-review process. You should know that it's *good* news when you receive a paper back from your professor that is covered in comments. You may not like it in the moment (I know I don't always like receiving peer reviewers' comments either), but your professor truly sees your potential as a writer and wants to help you improve in the same way an athletic coach would by giving you feedback on your performance.[24] In any case, professors feel your pain here because academic presses and journals only publish writings that have had their content scrutinized, commented upon, and (hopefully) approved by peer reviewers. We've all been through the same experience.

Not all works of nonfiction have gone through an academic peer-review process, and that's OK. Plenty of informative and useful works of nonfiction – like trade books, newspapers, and magazines – are published by reputable commercial presses without academic peer review.[25] Nevertheless, the fact that scholarly colleagues have not reviewed the content puts them lower on the hierarchy of source material than peer-reviewed sources. Despite this, the fact that these sources passed through some type of formal publishing process usually means that they undergo some type of formal editing. This may be limited to copyediting, depending on the publisher.

So-called tertiary sources sit at the next level down the source hierarchy. While some scholars place tertiary sources into an entirely different category, I tend to consider them as secondary sources. In any case, tertiary sources are collections of other secondary (and sometimes primary – hence the confused categorization) sources. The fact that they are not based on original primary-source research relegates them to the lower rungs of the evidentiary hierarchy. Encyclopedias, fact books, dictionaries, and usually textbooks are tertiary sources. Online encyclopedias like Wikipedia are also tertiary sources. Wikipedia can certainly be used to get a general overview of a topic (I use it too), but you should try to corroborate the information you find there. This means that Wikipedia and other tertiary sources, including your textbook, are never the strongest sources for your upcoming research paper. In fact, many professors will forbid you from using your textbook as a source altogether. This is because although textbooks are useful in helping you to understand a topic in a general way, they generally do not provide access to the types of primary sources that constitute the best evidence. Despite the fact that tertiary sources shouldn't be your main source for research projects, most print tertiary sources, especially those published by academic presses, have undergone at least some level of professional editorial review.

The sources with the lowest level of authority on the source hierarchy are secondary sources that have not undergone any type of review because they have been privately published or circulated. These may include self-published books, unpublished papers, websites, blog posts, and podcasts. Of course, these sources may still contain good information and arguments. For example, academics are increasingly uploading unpublished drafts of research or conference papers to websites like Academia.edu.[26] These can serve as valuable secondary source

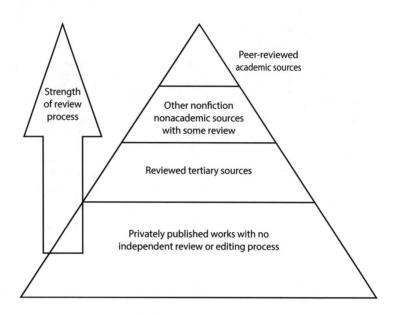

The Secondary-Source Hierarchy

material, but you'll need to do a little extra legwork to ensure the author and source are credible. We'll discuss what this legwork might entail shortly. As a rule of thumb, privately published materials can be usable, but you'll have to evaluate them very carefully.

Sometimes students worry about correctly categorizing sources as primary or secondary. This is especially true if the source is nontraditional or the answer is not so clear-cut. What about a mountain range, or example? What about a contemporary editorial blog post that quotes an eyewitness of a past event? There are questions you can ask to help yourself determine whether a source is primary or secondary. If the source is a text, you might ask how the author was able to write about the topic. Was he or she actually present? If so, then the source is probably a primary source. If the author wrote based on secondhand information, then the source is a secondary source. Did the author reach his or her conclusions by synthesizing or bringing together several different accounts of an event, person, or object? If so, this is a secondary source. Did the author reproduce a single direct encounter with an event, person, or object? This, then, is a primary source.[27]

The most important thing to remember is that the primary- vs. secondary-source distinction is merely a tool to help you better interpret sources. No source is primary as opposed to secondary in and of itself. Content and context matter. Additionally, you may well discover sources that are not relevant to your line of inquiry and therefore don't qualify as either primary or secondary sources for you in particular. Something only becomes a "source" once you've selected it as a relevant source of information. Nevertheless, being able to categorize sources helps us to ask more pertinent questions since we may need to look for different criteria when evaluating secondary as opposed to primary sources.

Exercise: Primary or Secondary?

Categorize the sources in the following scenarios as primary or secondary given the context, and say why:

1) You are an intrepid archeologist studying Viking settlements in northern Scotland.
   A. You dig up some human bones in an old Viking village and scientific testing confirms they originated in Scandinavia during the period of Viking settlement in Scotland. What type of source are these bones and why?
   Answer: The bones are a primary source because they were buried in an area of Viking settlement during the period under study.
   B. You write an article for a peer-reviewed academic journal that describes your findings. You succeed in having it published in a highly regarded journal. Congratulations! The article describes the Viking bones and makes an argument about the implications of your findings. What type of source is this article and why?
   Answer: The article is a secondary source because you wrote the article later to interpret past Viking settlements based on primary-source evidence.
   C. Along with the bones, you find some grave artifacts. You have them tested as well. They appear to have originated in Scandinavia and from the same time period

as the bones. What type of source are these artifacts and why?

Answer: They are primary sources because the artifacts were buried with the Vikings during the period under study.

D. Near the bones and artifacts, you find some iron objects. Again, you have them tested. At this point the lab decides to give you a bulk discount. The origin of the objects is unclear, and their design indicates that they were produced centuries later than the grave artifacts or the bones. What type of source are these objects and why?

Answer: The objects are primary sources for the era in which they were produced. They are not a primary source for the Viking period because they were deposited in the area *after* the Viking era. They are not a relevant secondary source for the Viking period either.

E. You decide to take a little vacation time while in Scotland and visit a local archive. There, you read a High Medieval manuscript that describes the Viking settlement of northern Scotland. The manuscript dates to several hundred years after the original settlement. What type of source is the manuscript and why?

Answer: It's an old secondary source for the Viking era. It's also a primary source for the High Middle Ages and therefore provides evidence of what people at that time thought about the Viking settlements. Historian Ludmilla Jordanova notes that these very early secondary sources are especially valuable since they are so much closer to the time under study than we are today.[28]

2. You are trying to learn more about the major earthquakes that occurred in Nepal in April and May 2015. After using Google, you arrive at a BBC news story titled "Nepal Earthquakes: Devastation in Maps and Images," from May 15, 2015 (http://www.bbc.com/news/world-asia-32479909), which includes text, a chart, maps, and photographs.

A. Is this news story about the earthquake a primary or secondary source? Why?

Answer: It's a primary source because it's reporting on a contemporary event. It may also include primary source material like quotations from eyewitnesses.

B. What about the component elements of the news story like the text, chart, maps, and photographs?
Answer: The text, chart, and photographs are primary sources. Charts have data, and photographs offer visual primary-source evidence of damage. Maps are interpretations of geography and therefore secondary sources.

C. You do another Google search and click on an article, titled "Lessons for Nepal, Three Years after Deadly Earthquake," that was posted on April 25, 2018 on the Human Rights Watch website (https://www.hrw.org/news/2018/04/25/lessons-nepal-three-years-after-deadly-earthquake). Is this article a primary or secondary source? Why?
Answer: This is a secondary source because it was written after the event to interpret it from a later perspective.

D. The article includes a photograph taken on April 21, 2017. Is this photograph a primary or secondary source? Why?
Answer: It is also a secondary source because it was taken two years after the event. But it is a primary source if you are interested in looking at lasting damage of the 2015 earthquake that is present in 2017.

CHAPTER 4

EVALUATING SOURCES WITH THE CRAAP TEST

The CRAAP Test

Now that we've gone over the distinctions between types of statements, and between primary and secondary sources, let's discuss a way to evaluate the sources themselves. Librarians and other information literacy professionals have been scrambling to come up with methods to help students better evaluate online sources, particularly given the rapidly changing world of the internet. When it's time to search for information on a topic, the first place to which students (or, increasingly, anyone) turn is Google. As you almost certainly know, after entering a search term into Google and hitting enter, a list of ranked search results appears in less than a second. But which source will be the most accurate? How do you know which ones to trust? University of Zurich professor Eszter Hargittai and other researchers have demonstrated that students tend to gauge a source's credibility based on its Google search ranking.[1] However, Google's algorithm does not take the critical evaluation of sources into account when spitting out its ranked results. Therefore, you'll have to do the heavy lifting of evaluating online sources yourself, just as you would at any other time.

But how can we evaluate these online sources or subject them to any kind of criticism? This may at first seem difficult, if not impossible. How can we determine currency if we can't date a website by sending ink out for an age-determining chemical analysis? How can we determine the identity and authority of anonymous authors on the World Wide Web? And if we can't necessarily determine who writes or publishes what on the internet, how can we determine bias?

Are we totally in the dark regarding online sources, to the point that they are unusable? No. It's true that the quantity of online material, combined with its ever-changing nature, makes the task difficult. But you don't need to be a skilled hacker with experience trolling through the dark web (a nebulous region I only vaguely understand myself) to evaluate online sources with the same critical intensity as traditional print sources.

The CRAAP Test:

- Currency
- Relevance
- Authority
- Accuracy
- Purpose

Librarians, historians, and others have been hard at work coming up with easy-to-use methods to help people better evaluate what they read, both in print and online. Several years ago, librarians at California State University – Chico's Meriam Library developed the aptly named "CRAAP test" to help readers determine the reliability of sources. Despite its colorful acronym – or because of it – the American Library Association (ALA) has embraced the CRAAP test because it helps students sniff out falsehood by asking them to consider five criteria: *currency, relevance, authority, accuracy,* and *purpose.*[2] "Currency" refers to the timeliness of the information source content. "Relevance" refers to whether or not the source content is relevant to your research needs or whatever topic with which you're engaging. "Authority" refers to who wrote the source and what his or her credentials are. "Accuracy" refers to the reliability of source content. Finally, "purpose" refers to why the author produced the source. What was the author's goal? What are the biases? While a number of methods (and acronyms) of source evaluation exist, and your professor may use a different one, none of them are really all that different. They may use different terms, and some combine multiple concepts whereas others divide them, but in the end, each method asks readers to look for the same things in sources. Since the CRAAP test both has a fantastic acronym that helps us remember our job – that is, to sniff out crap – and contains one of the most thorough lists of areas to assess, we'll use it in our discussion of how to evaluate sources. But remember that other methods are equally valid.

Currency

The first area of source assessment is currency. It's essential to know when a source was produced. "Currency" refers to the age of a source, or how current it is. Obviously, this can also help determine whether the source is a primary or secondary source in the first place. Knowing the publication date is important regardless of whether it is a primary or secondary source. All print journals and printed academic and trade books will include the date of publication. Remember that not all secondary sources are created equal. Scholars generally consider sources published more recently as stronger sources than older ones. The authors writing the closest to the present day have access to the most recent discoveries and data. In other words, they have the evidence necessary to make the strongest possible interpretation. They have also had the opportunity to revise earlier arguments or weed out factual errors and fallacies present in earlier secondary sources. The librarians at California State University – Chico's Meriam Library also note that you should consider currency in the context of your research topic. Some topics, like areas of active scientific research, may require the use of only very current sources. Others, like historical topics, may work with less current sources, provided they are classics in the field or make significant arguments. Nevertheless, as a rule of thumb, information literacy experts recommend current works over older ones regardless of the field.

When considering a source on the internet, it's extremely important to determine currency if for no other reason than not to look foolish. Periodically, stories that are years old start circulating on social media. Unwary readers assume that since the story is trending, it must be current. But that's not always the case! This seems to happen frequently with celebrity deaths. A major figure will pass away, and various media outlets will cover the news. Then a few years will pass and someone will share the story and you'll get a second massive outpouring of grief. For example, the BBC reported in 2016 that news had begun to spread across social media that the hilarious and beloved comedic actor Leslie Nielsen of *Airplane!* and *The Naked Gun* fame had passed away. Tributes rolled out across Facebook and Twitter. As it turned out, however, Nielsen had actually died in 2010 and had become the latest victim of what the BBC termed "Multiple Death Syndrome."[3]

Of course, with print sources you can check this problem at the door by simply looking at the publication date of an article. This may seem more difficult with internet sources than with print sources, since websites do not always publish a posting date. Nevertheless, the most reliable and authoritative sites, like those of newspapers and magazines or journals, do include dates of publication. If you are looking at a site that does not show a posting date, it may not be a very reliable source. Another factor to consider is that there is a difference among when the content of an online source was first written, was first posted, and was last revised or modified. For example, a professor may have written an essay in 2009 but only decided to post it on his website in 2017. Later, in 2020, he may decide to revise the same essay on the website. To complicate matters further, some websites automatically display the current date regardless of when content was created.

Determining online currency:

- Check site for dates
- Check to see if the date refers to authorship, posting, or last modification
- Check the Internet Archive for a last revision if you can't find a date
- Check to see if the hyperlinks are still working

In sum, check your sources for dates! Determine, if possible, whether the date listed is the date of authorship, date of posting, or date of the latest revision. If a website is going to include a date, it is most commonly the post date. Remember that when citing an internet source, you should ideally include the post date. If this is unavailable, you will need to use your access date. If a website includes no dates, you can use the Internet Archive to determine when it was last revised. The Internet Archive (https://archive.org/) is a nonprofit institutional member of the ALA dedicated to "building a digital library of Internet sites and other cultural artifacts in digital form."[4] It hosts the Wayback Machine, which uses automated web crawlers to archive and save internet sites and content. While not all web pages have been archived and saved, many have. As a result, you can use the Wayback Machine to determine the date that many websites were created and the last time web pages were updated.[5] Another trick to help you determine the age of a website is to click through the hyperlinks. If they no longer connect, that's a sign that the site may be out of date. In sum, do your best to determine whether a source is current by ferreting out the relevant date of publication. Sources without posted dates are often less credible.

Relevance

Once you have successfully established the currency of your source, you'll need to make sure it is relevant to your topic. You should ask yourself, Does this source contain information that is relevant to my topic or interests? So, if your topic is "gun control legislation in the state of Florida" and your source is a dancing kitten GIF, you've just failed in the relevance category, although you may have scored highly in the amusement category. Of course, things aren't always so clear-cut. If your topic is "the impact of fluoridation on dental health," a news story about a failed mayoral candidate from Grand Rapids, Michigan, who campaigned on ending water fluoridation is not relevant. While the story is interesting and mentions water fluoridation, its purpose is to inform the community about political news. As such, it would not provide relevant scientific data on the impact of fluoridation. As we can see from this example, part of evaluating the relevance of a source is determining its intended audience and goal. Is it meant for a popular audience interested in local political news? Is its primary goal to convey election results? Or is it meant for a scholarly audience interested in the analysis and interpretation of scientific data?

Determining online relevance:

- Is the source relevant to the specific topic?
- What is the source's audience and goal?
- At what level is the source written?
- Can you access the entire source and hosting website?

Moreover, is the source written at the appropriate level? A secondary source on fluoridation taken from a middle-schooler's blog would not be an appropriate source for an undergraduate-level research paper. Neither would a site on photosynthesis aimed at informing elementary school children. At the same time, an article from a major peer-reviewed academic journal might be too advanced for use in some – although by no means all – undergraduate contexts. A website hosting journal articles aimed at professional research scientists may be irrelevant to you simply because you still lack the knowledge to understand fully the evidence and language used in the sources. Moreover, as the Chico librarians remind us, you can't determine a source's relevance before examining several different sources. A source may appear to be more relevant than it really is before you've read other sources dealing with the same topic. Finally, in order to establish whether an online source is relevant, you'll also need to be able to successfully survey the entire hosting website. Can you easily access the home page? Ideally, the home page will include a link to an "about" section that will say more about the organization or individual that runs the website, which brings us to the question of authority.

Authority

Determining the author of a source or the publisher of a website will help you evaluate the authority of the author. Authority is a key component of the CRAAP test. In fact, now that access to online sources has largely cut out the intermediaries who used to ensure that the authors, editors, and publishers of sources had the proper qualifications, the ability to assess authority is more important than ever. In the wake of the moral panic over fake news in 2017, ALA president Julie Todaro called for more consideration of "the 'authority' component" of CRAAP.[6] When encountering a source you should first ask, Who wrote this? In some cases, you may ask, Who published or edited this? Reputable print sources usually include the author's name in an obvious location, like on the title page, on the first page of an article, or in a byline. On some websites, you may need to check an "about" section to find the author's name. Since the authority of authors and publishers establishes credibility, credible sources will usually include the authorship and contact information or a Twitter handle. Authors and publishers of credible sources also try to establish authorship as clearly as possible, whereas less credible sources may intentionally muddy the waters. Unfortunately, anonymity is much more common on the internet than it is in print sources. Anonymous sources, though, are something to definitely avoid.

After determining the author of a source, you will then need to determine whether the author's credentials make him or her qualified to write on the topic. First, examine the author's education or experience in the relevant area. For example, suppose you read a claim about vaccine timetables, which was a hot button topic in 2019 when measles outbreaks occurred around the United States. You read that individuals should delay receiving all vaccines until they are teenagers. Moreover, a family doctor with an actual MD made this claim. Should you accept this claim about vaccine timetables since someone who seems to have so much authority supports it? Not in this case. While the doctor in question does have some medical authority, general practitioners lack the education and credentials to overrule the unanimous authority of doctors and researchers who specialize in immunology and vaccines.

Determining online authority:

- Who wrote the source?
- Are the author's credentials relevant?
- What is the author's institutional affiliation, if any?
- What is the authority of the hosting website?

Even though the appeal to authority in the case above didn't pan out, appealing to authority is usually a good thing. Sometimes people with a little knowledge of informal logic will charge you with the fallacy of an "appeal to authority" if you try to bolster your position with evidence from an authority figure. This is only a fallacy if that authority figure lacks credentials in the relevant area. For example, having a PhD in microbiology does not make someone qualified to write on systemic theology. Nor does celebrity status as an actor qualify one to speak authoritatively on foreign policy issues. In contrast, appealing to the authority of the microbiologist when writing about microbiology, or the actor when writing about acting, is not fallacious.

In addition to checking the relevance of credentials, you should also be aware of the author's or editor's current position and institutional affiliations. These could be universities, think tanks, government bureaucracies or elected bodies, commercial enterprises, or nonprofit organizations, among others. If you are trying to determine whether or not an author has the proper authority to write on a given topic, it's helpful to know both the author's individual qualifications – Does she have the right credentials in the appropriate field? – and institutional context. For example, knowing that someone earned a PhD in economics tells you that she has demonstrated academic competence in that field. Further, knowing that a university employs her tells you that the accredited university has staked its own reputation on her authority and endorses her as an authority in economics. This is important because if the university "authorizes" someone unqualified, it risks losing its prestige, which could translate into the loss of student tuitions or grant monies. It's also important to note, however, that a great deal of excellent scholarship is produced by adjunct and contingent faculty. The lack of a tenure-track faculty position does not necessarily invalidate the authority of an author.

When it comes to online sources, you'll also want to check the authority of the website publishing the source. You'll need to be able to identify the publisher or responsible party. Although web pages do move, a site that moves around a lot should send up warning flags. You'll also need to make sure that the site is what it appears to be. Take, for example, a sensational story about a murder-suicide involving an FBI agent that was spread after being posted by the Denver

Guardian. The Denver Guardian certainly sounds like a real media outlet committed to publishing accurate news. In reality, though, the Denver Guardian, like the Boston Tribune and Baltimore Gazette, was a fake news site. The Denver Guardian was nothing more than a hastily thrown-together website consisting of a bunch of nonworking links and a fake street address, all created for the sole purpose of disseminating fabricated clickbait "news" stories.[7]

To complicate things further, individuals may use phony social media accounts or websites to impersonate a person or group and then to post fake news stories or messages. Of course, impersonation is often meant to be parody. In a comedy club, no one would confuse a stand-up comedian impersonating the president of the United States with the actual president. But since comedy is often lost in translation over the internet, some individuals do get fooled by comedic or satirical impersonations. Other sites, like Break Your Own News (https://breakyourownnews.com), allow users to create what appear to be images from a television news program broadcasting breaking news. Users can create their own, presumably humorous, fake news stories by uploading images, headlines, and phrases for the ticker. The resulting product can then be uploaded directly to Facebook or Imgur. Although the developers almost certainly intend their handiwork to be used for entertainment purposes, no doubt at least a few unsuspecting social media users will be fooled.

Aside from impersonations that are meant to be recognized as such for their comedic value, some individuals create fake accounts or bogus websites to intentionally fool people for more malevolent reasons. Examining who owns a domain can help you determine how authentic a website is. A website's address, or uniform resource locator (URL), can often tell you quite a bit about the site itself. The first part of a URL is called the protocol. This is usually the http or https part. The domain name comes after two slashes. The address's final period and the letters thereafter are called a domain suffix and represent the site's top-level domain (TLD).[8] Sometimes a URL includes additional text after the suffix. This takes browsers to a specific file hosted on the site's server. To give one example, in the University of Toronto Press's URL https://utorontopress.com/us/, https is the protocol, utorontopress.com is the domain name, and .com is the suffix. Remember that fake news sites often attempt to mimic real ones, like abcnews.com.co, run by Paul Horner, which shut down in October 2017. The actual ABC News site is abcnews.go.com. Notice that the phony site has a different suffix.

When it comes to social media like Facebook and Twitter, prior to 2018 many public figures used to be able to formally apply for verification badges that ensured the authenticity of their accounts. These appear on posts as white checkmarks inside blue badges. Today, this has created a bit of a complicated situation; many public figures retain their verification badge, but other figures with legitimate accounts are unable to get badges since the official process has been suspended. Therefore, while it's helpful to look for badges, the absence of a badge on a recent account doesn't necessarily mean it's bogus. Moreover, the presence of a badge doesn't always ensure authenticity either. Even if (especially if?) public figures post something exciting or controversial, even to verified social media accounts, you should still try to check the authenticity of the post by looking for corroboration from journalists or fact-checkers. This is because image manipulation software can also create phony verification badges.

Finally, some phony social media accounts on Twitter and other platforms aren't even human. Bots are software applications programmed to act like humans. In recent years, bot accounts have sprung up on a number of social media platforms. Creators design bots to deceive real people into thinking they are interacting with other real people. The purpose of this deception could be to sell products, to push a certain political line, simply to troll, or to spread misinformation. Disturbingly, recent research suggests that almost half of all tweets about the novel coronavirus derive from bots.[9] Bots are becoming increasingly sophisticated, but it's usually still possible to distinguish between a bot and a living human being. First, check the suspected bot's profile for anything suspicious, like a picture taken from another source. You can check by reverse image searching the picture. Second, examine the suspected bot's speech patterns. Is the language idiomatic? Of course, you could be dealing with a perfectly human nonnative speaker. Therefore, you should also look for repetitive phrases and the tendency to go off topic or repeatedly turn the discussion back to one specific topic. Check out the profile history. Constantly sending out heavily politicized – and often fake – news stories is typical bot behavior. Additionally, too many tweets in a

short period of time is often a sign that an account is run by a bot.[10]
If a Twitter account, for example, fails more than one of these tests,
it's likely you're dealing with a bot. If you're still not sure, websites
like Botometer (https://botometer.iuni.iu.edu/) can help determine
the probability that a Twitter account is a bot. Be sure to check so
you don't fall prey to the efforts of bot designers attempting to stir
up dissension on the web.

Accuracy

Like authority, accuracy is clearly an important component of
CRAAP – if you don't have accuracy, then all you are left with is,
by definition, CRAP. In order to determine the accuracy of source
content, we need to ask where the material came from and assess the
evidence. You should also ask whether the content has been subjected
to peer review. Moreover, can the content be corroborated? What
would you think if you read an online news article claiming Bigfoot
existed? Would you just believe it? I hope you wouldn't. You would,
hopefully, remember that anyone can publish anything on the internet and begin investigating the article's claims. First, you should look
to see if the article cites any reputable sources to back up its stupen-
dous claims about Bigfoot. In this case, I doubt it would.

What if the story is seemingly more plausible? Take the February 13, 2017, *New Yorker* story that education secretary Betsy DeVos
claimed that 40 per cent means more than half.[11] This story received
more than sixty thousand Google hits; undoubtedly, many assumed it
was factually accurate.[12] But several things should have raised warning
flags for readers. First and foremost, although the *New Yorker* is not
a fake news website, it does publish satirical humor. The story about
DeVos was written by humorist Andy Borowitz and clearly labeled as
his satirical "Borowitz Report." But secondly, supposing that Borowitz was attempting to pass off his essay as actual news, what were his
sources? Who heard DeVos say this? Where did she put this claim
into print? Proper citations and the use of credible sources to back up
claims is one of the most important indicators of accuracy. After all,
in order to make any claim, an author must have first received information from somewhere else.

That somewhere may be a secondary source or, better yet, a primary source. The strongest and most credible secondary sources are those that cite primary sources directly. You can think of primary sources as being like springs of information. That information flows out of the original sources and into secondary sources, which are like lakes. Information may also flow out of one secondary-source lake and into another. The most pure or credible secondary-source lake is usually the one that is closest to the original primary-source spring. Citations are like a map telling us how the system of lakes, rivers, and springs are connected. If you want to know where a particular claim came from – how it came to be floating in a lake – a citation will tell you. Perhaps it came from another lake, or perhaps it came directly from a primary-source spring. In either case, you'll want to follow up and investigate. Check the relevant sources cited by whatever article you happen to be reading. Websites generally use hyperlinks instead of traditional citations. Click on these links. Make sure that the lakes and springs listed on the map really exist. Unscrupulous content creators certainly could cite sources that do not really exist in order to give their site the appearance of credibility. This is a version of the *aesthetic fallacy*. Web designers could trick readers into believing a site contains accurate content by making it merely *look* credible. Remember also that it's not only text that needs citation. If an author uses data or other quantitative evidence, he or she needs to provide its source. Never just assume that numbers are automatically credible without figuring out where they came from. And if the author does not give you that opportunity because he did not provide citations, you should be skeptical. Providing citations, or listing the sources used, allows you – the reader – to determine if the evidence is itself credible.

Determining online accuracy:

- Are the source's claims plausible?
- Does it cite evidence?
- Are the citations clear and accurate?
- Has it undergone some review process?
- Is the hosting site reputable?

This type of corroboration to check accuracy is increasingly important because of the spread of fake news. Before believing anything you read, especially on the internet, it's wise to see first if you can find the same information in another source. Educators often make the mistake of getting students to focus so much on the source itself that they forget about the content. Given that determining the accuracy of source content is perhaps the most important component of source analysis, this is problematic.[13] Michael Caulfield of the American Democracy Project's Digital Polarization Initiative talks about this process of corroboration as reading "laterally."[14] Likewise, English professor Robert Harris notes that "it is a good idea to *triangulate your findings*: that is, find at least three sources that agree."[15] Caulfield and others also recommend both checking to see if a reputable fact-checker has already disproven a claim and using citations to trace claims to their source of origin.[16] Good fact-checkers include FactCheck.org, produced by the Annenberg Public Policy Center, and PolitiFact.com, a project of the Poynter Institute for Media Studies. Of course, it's important to remember that even fact-checkers cannot be perfectly unbiased. Moreover, some may be more intentionally skewed than others. For example, MediaMatters.org focuses on fact-checking conservative news sources, while NewsBusters.org focuses on checking liberal sites. For further fact-checking resources, look at the CUNY Graduate School of Journalism's excellent site "Fact-Checking & Verification for Reporting" and the ALA site "Evaluating Information."[17]

A Fact-Checking Exercise

Let's use the Annenberg Public Policy Center's FactCheck.org to fact-check some recent claims regarding the 2020 novel coronavirus pandemic. To use the site, click the search button and then type key words into the search bar.

1) The United States has overreported COVID-19 fatalities.
2) Face masks do not stop the spread of novel coronavirus.
3) The novel coronavirus originated as a Chinese biological weapon.

4) Flu shots increase a person's risk of contracting COVID-19.

5) Bill Gates predicted the outbreak of a pandemic several months ago during a simulation exercise. Therefore, he must be involved in the novel coronavirus pandemic.

Answers

1) A quick search leads to a relevant article, entitled "Social Media Posts Make Baseless Claim on COVID-19 Death Toll." Fact-checker Angelo Fichera writes, "Viral posts wrongly suggest that the COVID-19 death toll is exaggerated because 'the state' has instructed that 'anyone who didn't die by a gun shot wound or car accident' be listed as a coronavirus victim. Experts say there is no such default classification – and that the U.S. death count is probably underestimated."[18]

2) The article "COVID-19 Face Mask Advice, Explained" notes that scientists are split over the effectiveness of face masks. Moreover, the effectiveness of the mask depends on the type of mask worn and correct use.[19]

3) Searching tells us that scientists agree that the virus was not created in a lab as a bioweapon.[20]

4) Despite claims on social media, and in particular those made in a video entitled "Plandemic," experts agree that flu shots do not in any way increase the likelihood of contracting COVID-19.[21]

5) Back in October 2019, the Bill & Melinda Gates Foundation (along with the Johns Hopkins Center for Health Security and the World Economic Forum) hosted the Event 201 Exercise, which made policy recommendations regarding pandemics.[22] As a result, some reason that Gates had some role in the outbreak. There is no evidence of this.[23]

Obviously before accepting claims about COVID-19 or anything else, you should fact-check and see if you can find other news outlets reporting the same thing. If not, that's a sign that your source might not be factually accurate. In addition to using fact-checking sites, though, we should determine what type of source we are looking at. When it comes to print sources, you can usually tell what kind of editorial process they have undergone, be it academic peer review or grammatical revision. Websites, however, don't always clarify what, if any, editing has been done. Some academic sites – look for the .edu suffix – are peer reviewed and may announce this on the "about" page. Sometimes groups of academics found informal online journals or blogs that are peer reviewed but may have a .org or other suffix. Again, check the "about" page for more information. Documents published on education, government, or military websites appear under the authority of that institution and have generally been reviewed and endorsed prior to posting. Websites run by news organizations or publishers generally employ at least copyeditors. One way to tell if a website is not editing its content at all is to search for grammatical and spelling errors. Obviously, these can creep up even in peer-reviewed print sources, but they are more prevalent in sources that no one has edited. If you see several errors on a web page, avoid that site. Of course, again, just because a website that has few grammatical errors also looks professional doesn't mean the content is accurate. After all, it doesn't cost much or require much expertise to set up a good-looking website.

In sum, signs of content accuracy include plausibility, the use of evidence and citations, claims that can be corroborated, the use of peer review or posting material from peer-reviewed sources like books or journal articles, and a reputable hosting site. Grammatical or other errors may indicate a lack of peer or editorial review. But beware of the *aesthetic fallacy*. Just because a website looks academic doesn't mean it actually is. And speaking of fallacies, be on the lookout for emotionally charged language, which may indicate bias. Be sure that your own biases aren't impinging on your ability to determine the accuracy of an article, but also try to determine a source's bias. A strong bias may be a gateway to several informal logical fallacies like appeals to emotion, sweeping generalizations, *ad hominems*, among others. We'll talk about how to spot these later, but for now, just know that their presence seriously jeopardizes a source's accuracy and credibility. Finally, a source that includes only one side of the debate on a controversial issue and doesn't cite its sources may also be inaccurate or at least heavily biased.

Sources that are heavily biased may not be reasonable, which is something Harris argues we should also consider in a source.[24] By "reasonable," he means whether or not an author is even trying to produce an objective argument or report. Is there any attempt to limit bias? If an author is not reasonable, it damages the credibility of the source. Moreover, lack of reasonableness may also indicate that the author's purpose is not to objectively ferret out the truth but to reach a predetermined conclusion regardless of opposing evidence. Informal logical fallacies like use of immoderate language, ad hominems, exaggeration, and sweeping generalizations all may indicate unreasonableness.

Purpose

The issue of bias and reasonableness brings us to the question of a source's purpose. Determining purpose is important precisely because it helps us ferret out a source's possible bias. When students select a research topic, their first instinct is usually to do a simple Google search of a relevant word or phrase. The next instinct is usually to click on the most highly ranked website listed in the search results. But, as we have seen, Google's algorithms do not rank sites based on their accuracy or credibility. Nor does Google, or other search engines, ascertain a site's purpose.

The ability to access an "about" section of a website should help you to determine the purpose of a source's author. As a critical reader, you already know you need to identify the authors of online sources and ascertain their credentials and possible institutional affiliations. This allows you to determine their purpose. Ask yourself whether they are affiliated with an institution or are credentialed by an institution with a known ideological bias or purpose. If a libertarian think tank also employs our economics professor friend, it seems likely that her interpretations will lean in that direction. This does *not* necessarily mean that our libertarian economist would produce inaccurate content, but simply that we as readers should be cognizant of ideological bias. Biases aren't necessarily bad, and everyone has a bias, but part of being a critical thinker is acknowledging this and being aware of the biases that inevitably exist.

If the bias of an individual or institution is unclear, one way to check further is to see what type of funding your author or affiliated institution receives. For example, is the author of your source or the organization affiliated with your author funded by a liberal organization or by a right-wing think tank? One left-leaning online source that "tracks corporations" is the Center for Media and Democracy's site SourceWatch (https://sourcewatch.org/index.php/Source Watch). Of course, sites like SourceWatch are themselves biased. As noted, SourceWatch is a left-wing site dedicated to tracking companies that receive funding from perceived right-wing individuals and organizations. This *does not* necessarily invalidate the findings of either a funding tracker or your source itself (to argue that it did would be to commit the *genetic fallacy*), but it should make you pause to consider the possible bias.

If you are using an online source, you'll also want to examine the purpose of the hosting website itself. Look at the site's "about" section. If a site does not have a clearly labeled "about" or "contact" section, beware of the information presented. Even if you can't determine who runs a site from an "about" section, try to look for a hosting site. In either case, look for the mission of the website or the organization that owns the site. Is it to provide news as objectively as possible? Is it to provide access to peer-reviewed scientific papers? Is it a humor site? Is it an advertisement? It used to be the case that advertisements were fairly easy to distinguish from non-advertisements, but this is no longer the case, and research has shown that middle-school students have a hard time telling the difference. If a site is labeled as "sponsored content," that means it's essentially an advertisement, the purpose of which is to sell you something. Beware of information taken from such sites. A company trying to sell you something is obviously not going to give a rival company a fair hearing and will probably not present its content as objectively as possible. For instance, Coca-Cola is not going to write a sponsored article – really an advertisement – offering an objective comparison of its product with Pepsi.

However, a site could also try to do many things at once. Authors could be writing to make an argument, inform you, entertain, or sell something – or, in fact, they could be doing all those things. Authorial intent (that is, what the author is trying to accomplish) isn't like a person's birthday; you can have more than one. Nevertheless, it's still important to determine the author's primary purposes. If the primary purpose of an article is to sell you a new antibacterial cleaning solution, you ought to be critical of the author's scientific claims. This might not be a good source for a research paper on bacteriology. In any case, try to determine whether the author is clear or vague about his or her goal. If the author is vague, does this seem to be intentional?

Figuring out what the site is trying to accomplish is important because it is yet another way to help you determine the accuracy or credibility of the content. For example, there is not always a clear-cut distinction between deliberately false fake news, designed to trick readers, and factually accurate true news. There are also opinion-based websites prone to report events or make arguments in an exaggerated fashion owing to bias. Moreover, although all sites display some bias, the most credible sites attempt to remain as objective and neutral as possible. Less credible sites often display bias that is more open.

There are also satirical sites, such as the Onion and the Christian satire site the Babylon Bee. Most satirical sites explicitly state their purpose. However, not all sites are as clear about this as the Onion and the Babylon Bee. Some, like the Boston Tribune and the Denver Guardian, as discussed earlier, even take names that mimic legitimate newspapers. Many readers, especially those outside the site's target demographic, may miss the satire altogether and then share the stories as actual news. Or, as already noted, purveyors of fake news sometimes steal satirical content and then post it on their own sites as actual news. Therefore, before jumping to any conclusions about your source, it's important to determine its intended purpose. This is why it's so problematic for a site to be vague about its goals or mission.

Determining online purpose:

- Check the author's goal and bias
- Check the goal and bias of the author's affiliated institutions
- Check the goal and bias of the hosting website
- Check the source's language

Beyond checking a site's "about" section or mission to determine purpose, we can employ a few other techniques to ferret out possible bias. It's always a good idea to see what other websites may say about the bias or purpose of your source. So if you are using the *Wall Street Journal* as a source, do a little research on the *Wall Street Journal*. This will reveal that the newspaper is generally seen as politically center-right. Some organizations and individuals have also attempted to chart the political bias and reliability of news sources. Attorney Vanessa Otero, who founded Ad Fontes Media in 2018 to rank news bias and quality, has made one well-known attempt to do just this.[25] Otero first produced a chart to map out media bias in late 2016. Since then it has seen several updates, both major and minor; the most recent, interactive version is available at https://www.adfontesmedia.com/interactive -media-bias-chart-2/.[26] Otero's mapping work at Ad Fontes is overseen by an advisory board, which, if nothing else, prevents her efforts from lurching too far into subjectivity. Of course, Otero's chart itself has a bias – she openly admits to having a "moderately liberal bias"[27] – and therefore it's prudent to check more than one chart for such information. AllSides.com is a site whose staff, from a variety of political perspectives, seeks to rate media bias as left, left leaning, center, right leaning, or right.[28] Not surprisingly, AllSides produced its own Media Bias Chart in 2019.[29] Although we should be aware of its possible limitations, the Ad Fontes Media Bias Chart and AllSides Media Bias Chart are examples of places you could turn to get a sense of a major media source's political bias and quality.

When it comes to online sources, you'll also want to check the hosting site for its mission and possible bias. Just glancing at the domain suffix provides valuable information about who owns the site and what its purpose is. Common URLs end with .com, .org, .edu, .gov, and .mil. Each of these denotes a different type of website. For instance, .com denotes a commercial website, at least in theory. In practice the .com suffix has expanded to include websites affiliated with organizations that are not necessarily commercial as we usually think of that term. For example, many news websites also have a .com suffix. Nevertheless, the primary goal of many of these websites is to sell you something in order for the owner to make money. If you use a .com website, remember that the proprietor is possibly trying to sell you something. Websites with a .org suffix are owned by organizations

"AllSides Media Bias Chart," AllSides website, accessed June 26, 2019, https://www.allsides.com/media-bias/media-bias-chart.

including nonprofits. Just because these sites are not usually trying to sell you something for money doesn't mean they're not trying to sell you on their point of view. Be sure to examine these sites for bias as carefully as you would commercial sites. Additionally, although the .org suffix originated as a nonprofit suffix, that is no longer the case and many URLs with a .org suffix are not affiliated with nonprofits.

The .edu suffix indicates that a college or university owns the website. These are some of the strongest websites to use for research purposes. Since 2001, only institutions of higher education, which have been properly accredited, may use a .edu suffix. It is in the universities' best interest to post only academically sound and accurate materials. Nevertheless, you cannot turn off your CRAAP tester just because you see .edu at the end of a web address. University websites also sometimes host the private pages of associated students and faculty. As you probably know by now, mere affiliation with a university does not guarantee that a person always functions as a font of wisdom and unvarnished truth. Be on the lookout for the accuracy of these pages and any possibly inaccurate information. Finally, .gov refers to US federal, state, and local government sites, while .mil refers to US military websites.[30] These sites are generally more accurate than .com and .org sites because they frequently have greater levels of oversight and may post valuable primary sources, but, again, beware of institutional bias.[31] For example, a .gov website is unlikely to post documents critical of the US government.

But the suffix alone won't tell you everything. First, there is no "clearinghouse" authorizing domain purchases. Second, just think of how many different .com and .org sites there are. Sites with .com suffixes alone range from personal websites to news sites to sites selling soap. Therefore, we need to look beyond the suffix to determine a site's purpose. After examining the URL, it's worthwhile to find out who owns the site itself. You can look at the site's contact information, such as the publisher or email address. You can also investigate who actually owns a domain name or who is hosting it, by using one of several websites including https://www.whois.net, https://lookup.icann.org/, and https://hostingchecker.com. On one of these sites, enter the domain name in the search box and hit enter. They will often list the domain owner's registration information. Users can keep their information private, but some don't, which allows you to determine if a government organization or university owns a website as opposed to a private individual.[32] You should also check to see what other websites link to the site you are evaluating. You can do this by running a simple Google search with the name of your website.[33]

Another technique to which we've already alluded is to use the Internet Archive's Wayback Machine to see what the site used to look like.[34] The archive will often provide a summary of a website's changes over time and even breaks these changes down into screen captures, URLs, and new URLs in the site by text changes (text/HTML), jpeg/

The Wayback Machine at http://web.archive.org/

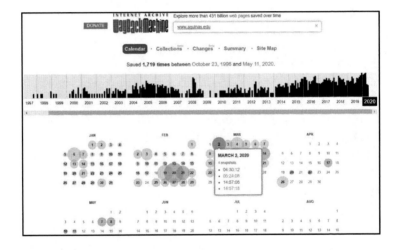

Enter a website. This example uses the website for Aquinas College (www.aquinas.edu). The Wayback Machine took four "snapshots" of the site on March 2, 2020. Click one to see what it looked like at that time.

images, and image/GIFs. It also shows how many times the site has been saved since being posted and the last time it was revised and saved.

Regarding some more purely digital tricks for determining purpose or bias, historian T. Mills Kelly notes that websites have used a variety of tricks to ensure the maximum number of visits to their pages. In the past, some writers recommended also paying attention to the way

On March 2, 2020 at 14:57 the website looked like this.

a website utilized "search engine optimization." Prior to the 2010s, this technique used so-called metadata like keywords inserted into the website's HTML source code to make sure that website showed up at the top of the search results. Search engines like Google once used words entered as metadata as part of the indexing and ranking process. Therefore, "when search engine users type in the same keywords, they are more likely to be routed directly to that page than if the metadata did not include those terms. For this reason, examining the metadata a website's creator(s) insert [could] offer useful clues to what sorts of search traffic they are trying to attract."[35] However, Google now trawls whole sites for keywords, not just metadata intentionally inserted into source code. As a result, although you'll still find relatively recent sources recommending this technique, it's no longer viable as an easy way to determine a site's purpose or target demographic.

Even if a source is not electronic, you can examine it for purpose based on language. Again, this is important because examining the bias can help you discern whether it has impinged substantially on the source's accuracy. One way to determine purpose or bias is to examine the source's tone, phraseology, and word choice.[36] For example, different sources may describe the same political speech as patriotic, nationalist, or jingoist, respectively. Each of these words has a different connotation. The word "patriotic" has more positive associations than the militaristic word "jingoistic," for example. The source describing the speech as patriotic, as opposed to nationalist or jingoist, is likely more biased in favor of its content. Additionally, you should examine the types of statements you find in your source. Are they opinions? Are they factual statements? Are there interpretations built out of evidence derived from other sources? If so, what are these other sources? Check the sources your source cites. Are these sources all or mostly biased in any obvious way? To what extent is the piece striving for objectivity? Sources striving for objectivity generally make better secondary sources than strongly biased ones.

In short, to determine the credibility of an online source, you'll need to examine its purpose and possible biases. Check the domain suffix and the mission of the particular site. Ask yourself if the goals and aims are intentionally unclear. Is a site meant to be obvious satire, like the Onion or the Babylon Bee? Is it satire that may intentionally confuse readers with its title or the appearance of its site? Does the site advertise something? Is the distinction between advertising and information on a website blurred? To what extent does a site seem to strive for reasonableness? Of course, just because a site is biased or even lacks credibility doesn't necessarily make it irrelevant as a primary source. For example, a source from the heavily biased American National Socialist Movement might be useful as a primary source if you were writing a research paper on contemporary American neo-Nazis. Just don't use a source from their site for a research paper on the Holocaust.

Now that we've finished our three-chapter survey of critical engagement with sources, let's take a look at how you might use the CRAAP test to evaluate a source. Suppose you are interested in learning more about recent US Supreme Court cases and come across an article entitled "Cakes, gerrymandering, Ginsburg and Thomas: Takeaways from a busy day at the Supreme Court" by Ariane de Vogue (https://www.cnn.com/2019/06/17/politics/supreme-court-takeaways /index.html). The article is dated June 17, 2019, and appeared on CNN's website in the "politics" department. How might we evaluate this source? We could start by asking whether it is current or not. In this case, since I'm writing this on June 18, 2019, this is a very current article, last updated only yesterday. It's also relevant because it deals directly with the topic we're researching. To check the authority of the piece, you should do a little research on Ariane de Vogue. Her byline tells us that she is a "CNN Supreme Court

Reporter." Clicking on de Vogue's name will take you to her CNN profile page, and a link on that page will take you to her full biography. You should also check for references to de Vogue outside of CNN's website. A Google search reveals a verified Twitter account and a verified Facebook page, among other things. Our research shows that de Vogue has the necessary credentials and expertise to write about the Supreme Court.

When it comes to accuracy, you should check the evidence that the source cites by clicking on the hyperlinks in the story. You should also try to corroborate claims by checking them against other sources. One place to do that in this case would be the official website of the Supreme Court (https://www.supremecourt.gov/). Finally, check the source's purpose. Is it trying to convince you of something? Persuade? Engage in neutral reporting? How about the website as a whole? Research the ideological slant of CNN. You may want to check out the bias charts I mentioned earlier.

A CRAAPpy Exercise

Now that we've had a survey of the CRAAP test, you get a chance to try it yourself. Suppose you are writing a paper on the American presidency in 2019. Your Google searches produce many possible sources. Of these, you select two articles. The first, by someone named Daniel Marans and entitled "Donald Trump's Political Arm Cites InfoWars in an Email Boasting about Crowd Size," appeared on June 3, 2017, in an internet newspaper called HuffPost (https://www.huffpost.com/entry/alex-jones-donald-trump-fundraising-email_n_593306d1e4b0c242ca249805).[37] The second, by someone using the pseudonym "Adam Mill" and entitled "7 Reasons 2019 Is Already a Terrible Year for Trump's Opponents," appeared on March 4, 2019, in an internet magazine called the Federalist (https://thefederalist.com/2019/03/04/7-reasons-2019-already-terrible-year-trumps-opponents/).[38] Before using these articles as sources in your research paper – or to make any kind of argument about the Trump presidency, for that matter – you should subject them to the CRAAP test or some version thereof to determine their credibility.

How might you determine your sources' currency, relevance, authority, accuracy, and purpose? Describe the strategies you would use to evaluate your source in each of these areas. Do a little research. Based on the above information and your own research, what can you determine about the CRAAP status of these two sources?

Source 1 ("Donald Trump's Political Arm Cites InfoWars in an Email Boasting about Crowd Size"):
    Currency:
    Relevance:
    Authority:
    Accuracy:
    Purpose:

Source 2 ("7 Reasons 2019 Is Already a Terrible Year for Trump's Opponents"):
    Currency:
    Relevance:
    Authority:
    Accuracy:
    Purpose:

Things to Consider

Consider the five elements of the CRAAP test: your sources' currency, relevance, authority, accuracy, and purpose.[39]

Currency: To determine a source's currency, you need to see when it was written and/or published. Remember that you're researching the Trump presidency in 2019. The first article is from 2017 and is therefore less current than the second article, which is from 2019. You might still check the first article to see if it was updated or revised in 2019. This appears to not be the case, however.

Relevance: Although one article is less current, both articles do deal with the Trump presidency. So in a broad sense both articles are relevant. Nevertheless, the first article covers only a very narrow topic and may not be relevant to a more general paper on the Trump presidency. The second article devotes a great deal of space to actors other than the president himself.

If you were working on an actual research paper, you'd also want to be sure these sources fit the assignment guidelines. For example, if your professor banned you from using internet newspapers and magazines, neither source is relevant.

Authority: To determine the authority of these sources, you first need to figure out who the authors are. The byline of each article gives their names.

HuffPost tells us that the author of the first article, Daniel Marans, "reports on the politics of the Democratic Party and progressive movements."[40] A search of HuffPost reveals that Marans has written numerous articles for the newspaper. His HuffPost reporter page also provides a link to his verified Twitter account (https://twitter.com/danielmarans). Maran's education and current reporting assignment can be found on his LinkedIn page (https://www.linkedin.com/in/danielmarans). He appears to be a credentialed and experienced reporter.

It is difficult to determine the authority of the author of the second article because he is using a pseudonym. You should always be wary of pseudonymous sources. All we know is that "Adam Mill" is an "attorney specializing in labor and employment and public administration law" who "has contributed to The Federalist, American Greatness, and The Daily Caller."[41]

Accuracy: How can we determine the accuracy of these two articles? We can start by checking the evidence cited in them. Internet news sources often do this via hyperlinks as opposed to traditional methods of citation. Click all the relevant links and see where they go. Broken links or links that land in the wrong place should function as warning signs. If the source doesn't cite any evidence, you should definitely at least question its commitment to accuracy and value as a source. Finally, you should try to corroborate any claims left uncited in your source. In the articles above, a little investigation reveals that some of the links in the first article ("criticized," "publishing," "FEMA camps," and "December 2015") no longer take you to the relevant site. The second article also has some broken links, such as the one attached to the word "security."

Purpose: Looking at the title and content of the two articles, what seems to be their primary purpose? Is it to inform? To persuade? A combination? We know that HuffPost, at least, classifies the first source as politics reporting based on the department in which the article originally appeared. The Federalist, likewise, classifies its article as politics. The purpose of the articles then is political reporting. However, this does not exhaust the purpose of either article. The title of the Federalist article, for example, illustrates reporting in the interest of political persuasion.

In addition to thinking about the purpose of the source itself, it's worth also thinking about the possible bias of these two online newspapers in general. First, we should note that given that lack of a .edu or .gov URL suffix, we can tell that these newspapers are not associated with either a credentialed institution of higher education or the government. Given that many media outlets use .com suffixes, the .com suffixes used by both HuffPost and the Federalist shouldn't raise too many eyebrows.

You should now consider the possible political bias of the articles. If you're not sure about this, you can always ask your professor. You can also turn to some resources we've discussed in this chapter, like the two media bias charts. In this case, the Ad Fontes chart ranks HuffPost (formerly the Huffington Post) as having a leftist bias and giving interpretations of the news that are between fair and unfair. This chart also ranks HuffPost as sitting between providing analysis and opinion/fair persuasion. The AllSides chart ranks HuffPost as left.

The Ad Fontes chart sees the Federalist as having a right-wing bias and sitting between fair and unfair interpretations of the news, although this chart puts the Federalist closer to the unfair category. The chart also ranks the Federalist as closer to giving unfair persuasion than HuffPost. Remember, though, that given Otero's liberal perspective, the Ad Fontes chart itself may be more likely than other charts to take a negative view of the Federalist. Meanwhile, the AllSides chart ranks the Federalist as right. In any case, thinking about the possible bias of the source can also help us get a sense of the intended audience or readership.

CHAPTER 5

READING YOUR SOURCES

Once you've evaluated a source, you'll need to really read it. This probably seems like an obvious thing to say, but I'm saying it anyway. In order to think critically about any textual source, you need to first be able to read it. Obviously, as a college student you are already a reader. One way you'll develop in college is by making the leap between merely reading with the knowledge of what words mean and reading for comprehension. You'll go from reading at a level beyond basic literacy to reading more critically. This will make the type of source evaluation we just discussed – not to mention most of your homework – possible. If the prospect of developing as a reader seems daunting, don't worry. Just like cooking or knitting, reading is a skill you can develop over time with practice and dedication to your craft.

Given that you are probably the least familiar with what we'll call academic texts, like textbooks or academic monographs, this chapter focuses on those formats. Moreover, of those two types of books, textbooks and monographs, you probably have a pretty good idea of what a textbook is. You probably read – or at least owned – some while you were in high school or a college class. A monograph, on the other hand, is most likely uncharted territory. An academic monograph is a (usually) peer-reviewed scholarly book that makes a specific argument. By definition, monographs are *nonfiction*. It's easy to slip into thinking that any big book is a novel. Just remember that novels are *fictional* by definition, as opposed to monographs. Related to academic monographs are peer-reviewed articles in academic journals. These are like long essays that make specific arguments. It's also worth keeping in mind that academic monographs (and journal articles) are nearly always used as secondary sources. Don't forget that a secondary source is an interpretation of the thing under study, not the thing itself or a direct account of the thing itself. In any case, this chapter will focus on reading secondary-source academic texts – but the basic strategies are also applicable to other texts.

Which House Are You Walking Into?

To become a better reader, you need to first know what you're getting into when you pick up a book or some other text. We could perhaps imagine the whole world of texts as a village composed of many different types of houses.[1] It might initially seem that any text can be read the same way, because, after all, they are all houses. However, this is not the case. A closer look at a village reveals that houses do differ; some are brownstones, some are ranch style, some are bungalows, and so on. If you stop to think about it, the same is true of texts. Text can appear within many, many different formats. There are academic monographs, textbooks, trade books, novels, essays, newspaper and magazine articles, blog posts, tweets, text messages, emails, and more.

Here we need to be realistic. Not all of these formats are equally easy to read. An academic monograph – at least partially because of the jargon and poor writing endemic among scholars – is almost always more difficult to read and comprehend than a newspaper article.[2] This is in part due to the fact that each of these is written for a different audience. Academic monographs are written for other scholars who are familiar with the jargon of their own tiny subspecialty and used to cumbersome prose. The newspaper article, on the other hand, is written for a lay audience and meant to be accessible to the general public. Moreover, whereas the writer of the monograph was primarily attempting to interest colleagues in his field, the author of the newspaper article probably tried to pull in a wider range of readers. As a result, most people are able to understand the newspaper article and read it more quickly.

Therefore, before you begin to read something, stop to consider what exactly it is you are reading. Obviously, you'll look at how many pages there are and probably how many images it contains as well. Don't worry, even professionals do that. But you should also consider whether the type of text you'll be reading is more like an academic monograph or more like a newspaper article. If it's an academic monograph, you'll need to set aside more time for reading and put more effort into understanding. Don't just blindly saunter into a textual house unawares like Goldilocks. First, stop to assess exactly what type of house you'll be walking into and what type of reading strategies you will need to employ.

Let's suppose now that you've entered the academic monograph house. Remember that an academic monograph is a peer-reviewed scholarly book that makes a specific argument. By virtue of picking up the book, or entering the house, you have some idea of the type of reading you'll do and what will be expected of you as a reader. You know that this type of reading will require more time and concentration than, say, a newspaper article or Reddit thread. You should read slowly, for understanding, and take notes. You may have already assumed all that. What other strategies are there for tackling a difficult academic book, essay, or article? Historian Heather Cox Richardson advocates a method that I have adopted with some success among my students. She argues that you should first read the introduction of a text. So far, so good. There is nothing too unexpected here, as we usually start reading at the beginning of a text. Then, however, Richardson may catch you off guard by telling you to read the conclusion next and skip the middle.[3] Why would you do this? As Richardson notes, historians and other academics usually lay out their main argument, or thesis, in the introduction and then repeat it in the conclusion. Therefore, the best way to get a grip on an author's argument is to carefully read the introduction and conclusion, even if your professor didn't assign them. Just because something isn't assigned doesn't mean you shouldn't read it.

How to Read an Academic Text:

- Read the introduction
- Read the conclusion or last chapter or section
- Go back and read the whole thing using the framing technique
- Consider which parts of a text are most important
- Consider how they relate to the argument
- Subject text to your own analysis

After having read the introduction and conclusion, it's then much easier to go back to the beginning and read the entire book. Ideally, the introduction and conclusion will give you a sense of what the author is trying to accomplish and his or her argument. This will form a framework within which you can make sense of the rest of the text. You might think of the entire book as a jigsaw puzzle. When I do puzzles – and I particularly enjoy the cat and flower thousand-piece subgenre – I always put the frame together first, as I imagine most people do. The edge pieces are the easiest to find and the simplest to put together thanks to having at least one recognizable straight edge. Then, after the frame is complete, it becomes much easier to figure out how the other pieces fit together, how one is related to another. The same is true of reading an academic monograph. Reading the introduction and conclusion helps you construct the book's or article's framing argument. Having established the argument, it is much easier to see how and why the individual chapters or sections hang together in relation both to each other and to the overall frame. As a result, the author's methodology, or method for arriving at his or her conclusion, becomes clearer.

In addition, as Richardson notes, we can actually repeat the framing strategy for reading a book on a smaller lever in each chapter or section of an article. For example, when reading a book chapter, try reading the first paragraph or so first and then the final paragraph or two. Good authors will lay out their chapter's main argument and how it relates to the overall argument of the book and other chapters at the beginning and end of each chapter. Many books will also include special headings within the chapter. Prior to reading the entire chapter all the way through, it's helpful to skim through and get a sense of what the author will argue on the basis of these headings.[4] Of course, not every book will have chapters with specially designated introduction and conclusion sections. Nevertheless, academic authors tend to write this way in practice. Additionally, be on the lookout for phrases like "I argue that," "in sum," "in conclusion," "I propose," "to sum up," or similar sounding expressions. Each of these indicates that the author is about to lay out the main argument or thesis, either for the first time, in the introduction, or for the last time, in the conclusion section. Our framing strategy can even work at the level of difficult paragraphs. You can read the topic sentence first and then the final sentence or two. This should give you a sense of what the author is arguing in the paragraph and how it relates to both previous and subsequent paragraphs.

Piecing together a text's frame also helps with a common concern students have about academic reading. Namely, they worry that they cannot possibly understand a text because it has too many strange names, dates, facts, numbers, etc. In other words, it is simply too full of unfamiliar stuff for them to understand. This concern stems from the assumption that reading comprehension is primarily about stuffing your head full of even more stuff. Students realize, correctly, that their brains have finite capacity. Moreover, they often assume that their brains always hover approximately a millimeter away from full capacity in the same way that the Doomsday Clock always seems poised just a few minutes prior to midnight. As a result, they fear that they cannot possibly read and understand a given book because all the stuff poured from the book into their brains will overflow, thereby making the entire enterprise ultimately futile. But these assumptions are incorrect.

The way to understand a text, and especially an academic text, is *not* to approach it like a big box of marbles. Students worried about information overflowing their brains see books as a box of marbles. Each fact or name or date or piece of information is like a marble, and *all* the marbles are perfectly identical. As a result, students have no way to order the marbles or know which marble is more important than the next. They assume they must simply stuff all the marbles into their brains and then fear that important marbles will accidentally fall out. But the marbles are *not* all the same. Knowing the author's argument helps you to know which "marbles" are more important than others. The marbles that most directly support the thesis or argument are the most important. We could perhaps imagine them as red. Marbles offering evidentiary support to the most important red marbles are of somewhat lesser importance. They could be blue. Marbles offering an even lesser level of support for the thesis could be yellow, and so on. As you read, use what you know about the author's goal and thesis to form a mental (or written) hierarchy of information and evidence. You can jot down the most important facts and note how they relate to the thesis. You can then take note of the relationship between other facts and theses. The most important thing is to recognize that not all names, dates, places, data, numbers, etc., in a book are equally important to understanding the author's argument. The wise reader will discern *which* are more important than others and spend her energy and precious brain space focusing on those. Additionally, the wise reader will focus on *how* a text's pieces fit together and support the overall argument.

While you read, then, you should be on the lookout for evidence. Evidence is what the author uses to support his or her argument. The names, dates, places, quotations, data, numbers, etc., that we discussed above, which perhaps are difficult to remember, function as evidence drawn from various primary and secondary sources. Ask yourself if the evidence is adequate or not. You can also be on the lookout for shoddy argumentation. Even if you use the techniques discussed in the previous chapter to determine whether your text made use of credible sources and reliable evidence, the author could still employ it in the service of bad arguments. We'll talk more about how to recognize logical fallacies later in the next chapter. Finally, as Richardson again writes, it's not enough to simply understand a book and then leave things there. What do you think about what you just read? You should be actively engaging with the author and text. You are now part of a conversation of sorts with the author across time and space. *Why* do you agree or not agree with the argument? What would you have changed? If you do entirely agree, has your thinking about this topic or others changed? Why or why not?

What I have just been saying about strategies for reading academic writing seems to assume all academic writing is the same. However, just as most houses these days do not consist of a single room, so too our textual houses, including the monograph house, consist of many different rooms. For example, suppose we briefly leave the monograph house and visit the village's novel house. In this house the rooms might represent different literary genres or subgenres. There could be literary fiction, detective fiction (my favorite), and romance rooms. But, to return to our academic example, the rooms in the monograph house could be the various academic disciplines. In other words, after entering through the front door, the room to your left could be the biology room. Walk down the hall and you'll find the English literature lounge. Climb upstairs and turn a sharp left and you'll enter the philosophy room. Keep ascending and you'll arrive at the history attic. To take our mental image further, we can imagine that the biology room will probably not look very much like the history room. There will be commonalities – both might have couches – but the interior design is probably quite different. Maybe the biology room is packed full of model DNA and the history room has lots of old maps. What's the point of this extended thought experiment? It is that just knowing whether you are reading an academic monograph or a novel isn't enough to make you a sharp reader. You also need to break things down further into disciplines, genres, or other subcategories of writing. Again, you should expect reading a work of biology to be something quite different than reading a work of history. If you tried to read a book about biology in the same way and with the same assumptions you would use to read a historical monograph, you would undoubtedly have a difficult time understanding the text. Certain features common in biology books (or rooms) might not appear in the history book, for example. As a reader, you want to know what to expect before walking into a room. Will you see model DNA or old maps? In other words, what types of evidence will the author likely use? Will the book contain experimental data or documentary evidence to support its argument? Knowing this ahead of time will help you make sense of what you read and know if the author has included adequate evidence in support of his or her argument.

Houses aren't often empty, though. They're full of people! In fact, we can imagine every one of our textual village houses as being filled with authors. So the academic monograph house is full of scholarly authors having a fantastic time chatting with one another. The literary scholars tend to hang out in the English literature lounge, the chemists usually congregate in the chemistry quarters, but folks can also mix and mingle. Music plays lightly in the background, the drinks are flowing, the conversation is lively; it's a great party! Don't you want to join? Lucky you! You *are* invited. Every time we read anything, we're entering into an engrossing conversation with the author of our piece and other authors who have written on the same topic. This brings us to the observation that, ideally, you don't simply enter a room full of people happily chatting away at a party and stand by yourself off in a corner.

Instead, you eventually – although perhaps more slowly if you're an introvert like me – enter into one of the many smaller conversations that are happening around the room. These conversations are the subjects or topics authors have written about within their various disciplines. So, for example, in the philosophy room there's a group of people engaged in animated debate over ethics. In the biology room there's a group more calmly discussing genetics research. Each author in the room is talking to other authors about his or her subject matter. And this is just what is happening in either an explicit or implicit way in virtually every piece of written text. Nothing is written in isolation. No man, nor text, is an island, as the poet John Donne would say. If you were really at this party, part of being a good listener would be understanding what the group is talking about and then what the positions of the various speakers are. This is equally true of being a good reader. You'll need to understand what subject matter the author is writing about. That's the conversation, so to speak. But the author is always in at least implicit conversation with others. Therefore, you'll also need to consider these other conversation partners to understand what exactly the author is claiming.

Subject and Goal

Once you've entered the conversation, you'll need to know how to follow it. First, as noted above, you'll want to figure out the subject of the conversation. This is simply the topic. Knowing which room of the academic house you're in can help you figure this out in a very general way. For example, you may know that a certain book is about history. You can learn even more about a book's subject by reading the title, as simple as it sounds. Oftentimes the titles of academic books are structured like *Something Catchy Sounding: The Actual Topic of the Book*. For example, the book title *Liberty or Death* doesn't give much information about the book's topic beyond it being somehow related to themes of liberty and death. You may even suppose the book is about the American Revolution, given the seeming reference to the famous speech given by the colonial revolutionary Patrick Henry in 1775. Closer inspection, however, reveals that the second part of the title *Liberty or Death*, after the colon, is *India's Journey to Independence and Division*.[5] Now you know that the book's topic is really the Indian independence movement and partition of 1947. After reading the title, you'll probably dig into the book's introduction. This should make the topic even clearer, if it isn't already clear.

Once you've got the topic of a book or article nailed down, you'll need to consider the author's goal. In academic writing, the author is always striving to answer a question of some kind. Students often confuse the subject or topic of a piece of writing with its goal. The subject is what the book or article is about. The goal is what the author is trying to accomplish by writing about that topic. For example, a topic might be the American Revolution. An author's goal might then be to determine why fewer than half of the colonists supported the cause of independence. The goal then is something an author is trying *to do* or *to accomplish*. Be on the lookout for "to" language to determine what the author's goal is. Naturally, authors aren't always so explicit, but nevertheless, all good academic writing sets out to accomplish something. It's your job to read carefully in order to determine what it is. If you are unaware of what the author's goal is at the outset, it will be difficult for you to follow the rest of the textual conversation.

Thesis

The most important part of nearly all academic writing is the thesis. This thesis is the answer to the original question posed by the author. Another way to think of a thesis is as the argument an author is sustaining throughout a piece of writing, or "conversation," so to speak. Sometimes authors are very direct, explicitly stating their theses in a single sentence or two. Other times they are indirect and you'll need to discover an implicit argument. As mentioned earlier, whether the thesis is explicit or more implicit, you can usually find it in a book's introduction or first chapter and again in the conclusion, if there is one. Yet, you still may not be entirely clear about what a thesis actually *is* beyond having a vague sense that it's an argument or an answer of some kind. When I ask students to identify an author's thesis, they often have a difficult time doing so. In fact, this can be the most difficult part of critical reading. And yet it is also the most important. It might help to think about what a thesis is *not*.

First, a thesis is *not* the same thing as the subject. The subject is the topic the author is writing about, as we have seen above. The thesis, on the other hand, is the argument an author is making about some aspect of that subject or topic. For example, the author may be writing about the 1947 partition of British India. The subject is the partition itself. The thesis may be that earlier attempts by the British government to harm the Indian independence movement by pitting Muslim and Hindu nationalists against each other was a major factor in the eventual division of British India into the Republic of India and Pakistan. Note that someone could hypothetically argue *against* the idea that British actions were a major factor in the 1947 partition. If what you identify as the thesis of a book or article cannot be argued against, then it isn't a thesis. Instead, it may simply be a restatement of the subject matter. In this example, if the author says he's writing about British India and its partition, that's the subject, not the argument.

Second, a thesis is *not* a goal or a question. Students often confuse the *goal* of an article or book with its *thesis*. I find that this happens much more than confusing a work's subject and thesis. Remember that the goal is what the writer is trying *to accomplish*. Again, another way of thinking about this is that the goal of a book or article is to figure out the answer to a scholarly question. For example, a goal might be to determine what caused the partition of India. The thesis would be the conclusion the author arrives at after doing extensive research. So the thesis is always the *answer* to a scholarly question. It is *never a question*. If you pick out what you think is an author's thesis but it can be phrased as a question, then it's not really the thesis. It's the goal or the question being asked. The thesis is *always the answer* to the question. In our Indian example, after asking what caused the partition, the author might determine it was British attempts to play Hindu and Muslim nationalists off each other. One example the author could cite in support of this thesis might be the earlier 1905 Partition of Bengal under Lord Curzon. In any case, the thesis is what the author *concludes* or *determines* was the cause of the partition.

Major Aspects of Academic Writing to Identify:

- Subject
- Goal
- Thesis
- Methodology
- Context or place in the historiography or scholarly literature

Finally, a true thesis cannot be merely a statement of fact. "British India was partitioned into the Republic of India and Pakistan in 1947" is a statement of fact and therefore not a real thesis. A thesis must be an interpretation or argument based on evidence that is open to debate. Statements of fact are usually not open to debate. Unless you have the capacity to fly back to 1947 in a time machine and undo the partition of India, what happened is set in stone. Therefore, when you are trying to determine an author's thesis, remember that something is only a thesis when a counterargument is possible. Related to this, when you are evaluating a piece of writing bear in mind that there can be stronger theses and weaker theses. A thesis is stronger the more specific, unique, and debatable it is. An argument that British activity in India changed the course of Indian politics is not a very good thesis. Why not? Because this is so little more than a statement of fact that it would be difficult to mount a reasonable counterargument. If the argument you identify as an author's thesis is extremely vague or not much more than a statement of fact then either you have misidentified the thesis or you have identified a weak thesis. In the latter case, take note that one way the author could have improved his or her work is by writing a more specific, more argumentative, and therefore stronger thesis.

Methodology and Literature Review or Historiography

Once you've determined what an author is arguing, what the thesis is, you should begin trying to determine the relevant methodology. This may sound complicated, but really an author's methodology is just the method he or she uses to move from question to answer. In other words, *how* did the author answer his initial question? This brings us back to the issue of sources and evidence. When reading, you'll need to consider what types of sources the author used. Ask yourself, are these credible sources? Here you'll employ the skills we discussed in the previous chapter. Then ask yourself how the author analyzes the sources. For example, does he employ qualitative analysis? Quantitative analysis? Perform a scientific experiment? Besides sources, you should also pay attention to how an author structures his argument. Does the author structure his arguments chronologically or thematically? In any case, while reading – or, to return to our conversation analogy, when listening – pay attention to *how* the author makes his case.

Finally, as already alluded to, people don't generally just talk – or write – into space. They either explicitly or implicitly join a conversation with others about a certain specific topic. This means that when reading a text you will miss much of the meaning if you fail to acknowledge the relevant conversation partners. Especially in the introduction, but also through a book, pay careful attention when an author mentions other scholars or books by name. These are the conversation partners. The purpose of mentioning these other writers is usually so an author can distinguish her own position from that of others. Or, on the other hand, an author may want to say that she agrees with what someone else has written on the topic in the past. This "compare and contrast" between what a scholar will write and what others have already written helps to bring out a book's argument more clearly. Therefore, understanding when an author is comparing her work with another work can also help you, the reader, make more sense of what you're reading.

The term historiography refers to the history of scholarship written about a topic. It also refers to the methods scholars have used to write about a given topic.

Of course, an author may not name names, so to speak. Sometimes an author will compare or contrast his argument with other arguments and the reader is expected to already know who the other conversation partners are. This makes it difficult when you are new to the conversation. But don't despair. The longer you involve yourself in any given conversation by reading about a topic, the more you'll understand the different arguments and various participants. Moreover, you can always ask your professor to help you identify the names and arguments of only implicit conversation partners. It's worth noting that on occasion an author may identify a gap in the historiography, meaning that he or she is about to write about a topic or make an argument that has not been written about yet. If this is the case, ask yourself if this is actually true. It might be worth doing a little additional research to find out. At this point in the reading process, you're ready to make your own – possibly unique – contribution to the discussion.

Part of your own contribution may even be critiquing the book or article you are reading. This is all part of active reading or listening. Once you determine the author's subject matter, goal, main argument (thesis), methodology, and how she is interacting with the arguments of other writers, then you can make an informed analysis of a piece of writing. To keep track of all these different things, it may help to annotate your book or take notes while reading. Underlining and highlighting can also be helpful. But whatever you choose to do, the point is to keep your mind actively engaged with what you are reading. Think of questions to ask about what you are reading. For example, is the author's goal appropriate to the subject matter? If the subject is India it wouldn't make much sense for the author to aim to uncover the causes of the Meiji Restoration in Japan. Is the goal reasonable given the length of the piece of writing? For example, is it reasonable to expect that an author can adequately explain the theory of special relativity and its possible relationship to Cubism in a three-page article? What about the thesis? Is it sufficiently argumentative? Does it actually answer the question? If an author's goal is to determine what caused the partition of India and her answer is that General Lee lost at Gettysburg, then there's a mismatch.

What about the methodology? Is the evidence used appropriate to the question asked and does it support the ultimate conclusion? Were the sources credible? Remember the CRAAP test. Finally, does the author interact with the arguments of other authors in a respectful and responsible manner? As far as you can tell, does he present their arguments accurately, or is he battling straw men? Does he even bother to position his argument vis-à-vis those of others? In academic writing, this is an important part of establishing one's own unique argument and voice in the scholarly conversation. Asking these questions, among others, will help you read actively and enable you to make an informed critique of academic writing. And doing this will help you distinguish falsehood from truth in the process.

Writing Workouts to Enhance Reading Comprehension: Précis, Abstracts, and Summaries

Précis and Abstracts

One good technique for enhancing your reading comprehension of academic monographs and journal articles is writing précis.[6] "Précis" is a funny word. It's pronounced pray-see and looks the same whether it is singular or plural (pronounced pray-seez). It is also a type of writing assignment you may encounter in a class. In fact, if you go on to graduate school in many fields, you will probably find yourself writing something like a précis on a regular basis. A précis is a concise abstract or statement of a book's or article's goal, argument, methodology, place in the historiography, and main points, as well as your analysis. Some professors may refer to these as book review assignments or by another name. Why do professors assign précis? Isn't it redundant if you're mostly just restating the contents of the assigned book? Writing a précis forces you to be a critical and active reader. You will need to think deeply about the book's goals, methods, and arguments. In particular, you will need to keep the book's thesis constantly in mind and consider how the author uses evidence to support an argument.[7] Writing précis is also an excellent way to learn to write in a concise format.

As historian Mary Lynn Rampolla notes, there is no one universal right way to write a précis, but all précis should include a few basic elements.[8] The shortest and most concise type of précis is sometimes called an abstract. Abstracts of books or articles should explain the author's 1) goal, 2) thesis/argument, 3) methodology, and 4) place in the literature (i.e., how does he or she compare or contrast with other authors in the field). Length of abstracts can vary, but the abstracts I assign in my classes should be no more than one double-spaced typed page. If you have room on the page, I tell students that an abstract or précis could also usefully include a few sentences summarizing the content.

Some précis are slightly longer and should include your own analysis of the relevant book or article. Again, these types of précis are sometimes called book reviews or critiques. I just call them précis. Remember, there is no one perfect way to write one of these précis.

However, scholars will generally expect to see the same elements we have already discussed. When writing a précis of a book or article you should 1) state the author's goal, 2) communicate the thesis or argument in your own words, 3) explain the author's methodology and 4) place in the historiography, 5) briefly summarize the book's content or main points, and 6) offer your own analysis of the book's argument. Once again, concise writing is very important.

Let's break down those six elements a little further one more time. When writing about the author's goal, you should ask what the purpose of the book is. Be sure to determine what scholarly question the author is asking. When writing about the author's thesis, remember that the thesis is *always* the *answer* to the author's question. A thesis is never a question, nor is it the broader goal or purpose of the book. Determining the author's thesis is the most important part of a précis. When writing about the author's methodology, you will need to answer the question, *how* did the author make his or her argument? One of the most important things to consider is what type of evidence the author used to support the argument. When writing about the book's place in the wider historiography or relevant literature, you should compare or contrast it with other books in the same scholarly field. You can consider the author's argument or findings, methods, and philosophical framework. When writing the short summary portion of a précis, you should include only the most important points or categories of evidence. This is where it is especially important to be concise.

When writing the analysis or critique portion of a précis, students often write that a book or article was "good" or "hard to read."[9] These things may be true, but they do not exactly constitute the hard-hitting analysis your reader (i.e., your professor) is looking for. Instead, you might answer questions such as the following: Do you think the author makes a strong or weak argument based on the evidence presented? Do you think a different methodology would have worked better? What presuppositions or biases does the author have and how do these influence his or her work? Finally, if you find yourself writing a précis for a class, your professor may ask you not to write in the grammatical first or second person. This means do not use "I," "me," or "you." For example, do not say "I think this book's thesis is ...." Instead, write "This book's thesis is ...." The reader will know you are the one determining the thesis without you explicitly saying it.[10]

Summaries

Instead of (or in addition to) précis, some professors assign written summaries of textbook chapters as part of their courses. I have been known to do this myself. Initially, some students resent this because it seems like busywork. However, I assure you, professors do not want to read and grade busywork any more than students want to write it. Therefore, none of the writing assigned by your professors is busywork. Why write summaries of secondary sources then? Simply put, writing summaries forces you to be an attentive and active reader. Writing a summary, which is usually quite short, is more thought-intensive than it looks. Writers need to read an article or book chapter in such a way that they *understand* the main point or argument. They also need to understand *how* evidence and examples are deployed to support that argument. Then, the student writer needs to condense all this down to a summary that may be no longer than a single page. As a result, it can usually include little more than the main point and the most important examples. As Rampolla notes, "Writing a summary requires you to condense what you have read and describe the author's central ideas in your own words; it helps ensure that you have understood and digested the material."[11]

Writing summaries, then, forces you to read actively and really think about what you are reading. The reason professors assign summaries is so that you will better understand the material and be better prepared to engage in intelligent discussion with your classmates. Surprisingly enough, students have often written on my course evaluations that, in retrospect, writing summaries was one of the most valuable parts of their class experience. I can only assume this is because writing does indeed lead to critical thinking and understanding. It is important to note, though, that a summary is different than a précis. A summary requires you to understand and reproduce another author's argument in a synthesized and condensed format. A précis requires you to also critically analyze the text.[12] Now that you know how to write both précis and summaries, you don't need to wait for an assignment from your professor to practice. You can use these techniques on your own to help you better understand what you read and to prepare for class discussion. The next time your professor assigns a particularly dense book, try to write a précis or summary. The extra work you put into writing it will almost certainly be rewarded with greater comprehension.

Critical Reading Exercise #1

Based on this excerpt from a journal article I wrote in 2014, can you identify my subject, goal, thesis/main argument, how I try to position myself relative to other scholarly work on the subject, and methodology?

> Joseph Conrad, Thomas Hardy, H. G. Wells, Samuel Butler, and Guy Thorne: which name does not belong with the rest? Of course Guy Thorne is the name that stands out today. Conrad, Hardy, Wells, and Butler are easily recognizable as Transition era authors. Yet Thorne was also not only a novelist but for most Edwardian Britons probably the best known. Despite being wildly popular among his contemporaries, Thorne is largely forgotten today in scholarly circles. When he is remembered, it is usually as the author of the bestseller *When It Was Dark*, published in 1903. Since *When It Was Dark* tells the story of a Jewish millionaire who attempts to destroy Christianity, it is not surprising that scholars have seen the work primarily in light of anti-Semitism. Nevertheless, such readings of *When It Was Dark* fail to take the work seriously on its own terms and examine the historical context within which Thorne worked.
>   Guy Thorne (1876–1923), born Arthur Edward Ranger Gull, was a journalist, sportsman, avid drinker, man-about-town, and a committed Anglo-Catholic. Like many of his contemporaries, he was caught up in the so-called "Great Church Crisis," a conflict between the Protestant and Catholic parties within the Church of England occurring between 1898 and 1906. A close reading of *When It Was Dark*, combined with Thorne's own statements and those of his contemporary readers, reveals that its polemics were not primarily directed against Jews or Judaism, but against radical anti-Catholic Protestantism – a forgotten early twentieth-century moral panic and a significant preoccupation of late-Victorian and Edwardian popular literature.[13]

Answers

Subject: The author Guy Thorne and his novel *When It Was Dark*.

Goal: To test whether the most common interpretation of *When It Was Dark* as primarily an anti-Semitic work holds up by reading the book in the context of contemporary religious upheaval.

Thesis/main argument: *When It Was Dark*'s "polemics were not primarily directed against Jews or Judaism, but against radical anti-Catholic Protestantism – a forgotten early twentieth-century moral panic and a significant preoccupation of late-Victorian and Edwardian popular literature."

How the author positions herself relative to other scholarly work on the subject: "Despite being wildly popular among his contemporaries, Thorne is largely forgotten today in scholarly circles. When he is remembered, it is usually as the author of the bestseller *When It Was Dark*, published in 1903. Since *When It Was Dark* tells the story of a Jewish millionaire who attempts to destroy Christianity, it is not surprising that scholars have seen the work primarily in light of anti-Semitism. Nevertheless, such readings of *When It Was Dark* fail to take the work seriously on its own terms and examine the historical context within which Thorne worked."

Methodology: This article attempts "to take the work seriously on its own terms and examine the historical context within which Thorne worked." It also uses a "close reading of *When It Was Dark*, combined with Thorne's own statements and those of his contemporary readers."

Critical Reading Exercise #2

Based on this excerpt from a journal article I wrote in 2018, can you identify my subject, goal, thesis/main argument, how I try to position myself relative to other scholarly work on the subject, and methodology?

When I asked my general education history students to introduce themselves, one announced that he had worked on the Donald Trump presidential campaign. I glanced around the room to gauge reactions. A few were affirming. Most were decidedly not. This, I thought, could be an extremely interesting semester, and it was, because it forced me to think more critically about how Roman Catholic higher education, specifically in the general education classroom, can contribute to our students' ability to refine their own intellectual commitments through interaction with those holding opposing worldviews. Of course, if we are dedicated to educating for the common good – and Catholic institutions must be – then we must also consider how to ensure that such interactions contribute to a more peaceable and just society.

General education curricula at Catholic colleges function as a training ground for refining the mindset and skills students will need to navigate post-graduation life in a pluralist world. What, then, should we expect from the Catholic general education gymnasium of the mind and soul? First, course content must allow students to better understand existing social, political, cultural, and religious conditions. This creates the knowledge necessary to successfully negotiate and appreciate diverse contemporary environments. Second, students should encounter the alien worldviews of both living individuals and historical actors. This creates "provocative encounters" that enable students to refine their own worldviews. Finally, students should be asked to interpret the pluralistic world of the present and past from the perspective of their own worldview commitments. This allows them to develop the skills and dispositions needed to best engage and serve neighbors of differing worldviews in order to contribute to the common good.

As a potent practical example, this article concludes by exploring how teaching the history of the Protestant Reformation(s) in a general education history class can achieve our desired student learning outcomes. The 500th anniversary of the Protestant Reformation in 2017 occasioned a series of celebrations, commiserations, and other forms of remembrance throughout the world. Roman Catholics and their institutions, in particular, may have been conflicted over how to respond. Should the Reformation be highlighted or ignored? Moreover, the quincentenary of the Reformation arrived at a time of intense soul searching among academic administrators and faculty alike. In some areas, private, liberal arts colleges find themselves increasingly forced to justify their general education curricula while competing for an ever-shrinking number of high school graduates.[14]

Answers

Subject: General education classes at Catholic colleges existing in a pluralist world in which not everyone is Catholic.

Goal: To determine (or at least explore) how general education classes at Catholic colleges "function as a training ground for refining the mindset and skills students will need to navigate postgraduation life in a pluralist world." In other words, what mindset and skills should these classes seek to impart?

Thesis/main argument: "First, course content must allow students to better understand existing social, political, cultural, and religious conditions.... Second, students should encounter the alien worldviews of both living individuals and historical actors.... Finally, students should be asked to interpret the pluralistic world of the present and past from the perspective of their own worldview commitments. This allows them to develop the skills and dispositions needed to best engage and serve neighbors of differing worldviews in order to contribute to the common good."

How the author positions herself relative to other scholarly work on the subject: I do not explicitly mention this in the opening paragraphs, although the phrase and concept of "provocative encounters," which informs much of this article, comes directly from the work of Matthew J. Mayhew and Alyssa N. Rockenbach.

Methodology: "As a … practical example, this article concludes by exploring how teaching the history of the Protestant Reformation(s) in a general education history class can achieve our desired student learning outcomes."

PART II

FALLACIES

CHAPTER 6

EVALUATING THE CONTENT OF SOURCES – FALLACIES OF CAUSATION

Formal and Informal Fallacies

Now that you've filtered out falsehoods, what about fallacies? Fallacies are not errors per se. Rather, they are bad arguments or pitfalls that can lead to erroneous conclusions. I hope that you either have had or will have a philosophy course in logic at some point in your college career. In fact, one of the things I most regret about my college education is not having had the opportunity to take such a course. This is because understanding the discipline of logic can help you better identify the many bad arguments you will encounter, think critically, and strengthen your own arguments.[1] Although we don't usually think of them this way, arguments themselves consist of a logically connected chain of statements, called premises, and a statement that *follows* from the premises, called a conclusion. These premises and the relation of their terms constitute the evidentiary basis of the argument. As educator Robert Gula notes, "if the conclusion does indeed logically follow from the premises, the argument is *valid*; if the conclusion does not logically follow from the premises, the argument is *invalid*."[2] The technical terms "valid" and "invalid," then, pertain to the logical form of the argument, not to the particular truth values of its premises and conclusion. A valid argument is any argument form where the premises are logically related such that, if the premises are true, then the conclusion is necessarily true. In a valid argument form, it is impossible for the conclusion to be false given the truth of the premises. On the other hand, an invalid argument is any argument where the premises are logically related such that is possible for all true premises to result in a false conclusion.[3] In a valid deductive argument the conclusion follows from the premises with necessity, whereas the conclusion does not necessarily follow in an invalid argument. Moreover, untrue evidence (false premises) will yield what philosophers call an *unsound* argument or conclusion. When evaluating an argument to determine whether it is sound or unsound, then, take into account the truth value of the particular premises. Sound arguments are valid arguments that also have true premises. In other words, in a sound argument, the premises are true and they logically lead to and necessitate the conclusion.[4] In addition to thinking of arguments as invalid or valid and unsound or sound, we can also think of them as possibly containing formal or informal fallacies.[5]

A formal fallacy involves an error in an argument's structure, or how it is constructed. An informal fallacy involves an error in the content of an argument.

Philosopher Jacob Van Vleet explains the difference by pointing out that formal logical fallacies exist because of an error in the argument's very form. We could also think about this as an error in deductive reasoning. Precisely, formal fallacies are invalid forms of deductive reasoning where the premises are *taken* to necessitate the conclusion but they cannot logically accomplish this, as it is possible for these argument forms to have all true premises and a false conclusion.[6] More often than not, however, you will encounter informal fallacies, which are errors in the content of the argument.[7] When evaluating sources and reading critically you should obviously be on the lookout for both kinds of logical fallacies. However, content errors or informal fallacies tend to generate most of the bad arguments in contemporary news stories, articles, essays, and even books. Your task as a student and citizen is not only to evaluate sources themselves but also to evaluate their content. A source may be legitimate, but does it contain arguments with a flawed structure? Or does the presence of untrue or weak evidence lead to a jumble of informal fallacies? With fewer and fewer intermediaries between you and the sources, it's up to *you* to make that determination.

In an effort to help you identify and proactively filter out these fallacies – both formal and informal – I've highlighted several common ones over the course of the next few chapters. I've broken these into several different categories, and it's worth noting up front that fallacies can fit into more than one category and can be grouped in any number of ways.[8] In other words, don't make the mistake of thinking these categories are anything more than one helpful way of thinking about or grouping different individual fallacies by shared characteristics. Other people categorize formal and informal fallacies differently and that's fine; there's no one accepted method.

Formal Fallacies Related to Causation

Non sequiturs

Let's start by examining some common fallacies related to causation. As a historian, I spend a lot of time thinking about causation, so this strikes me as a good place to start. We'll spend most of our time in the next chapters looking at informal fallacies, but there are a few formal causal fallacies you may encounter as well. Many of these are so-called non sequiturs, in which the conclusion does not follow logically from the premises.[9] A non sequitur appears to present a causal relationship between two things. But, upon closer investigation, there is really no cause-and-effect relationship at all, hence the term "non sequitur," a Latin term that means "does not follow." This is a useful concept to know. For example, one could attempt to argue that we want our college to be as sustainable as possible; therefore, our college mascot is a dog. What? Non sequitur! The conclusion about the college mascot being an anthropomorphic Saint Bernard does not logically follow from a premise about zero waste production.[10]

The gambler's and hot hand fallacies are specific types of non sequitur fallacies. The *gambler's fallacy* gets its name from the propensity of gamblers to fall prey to its wiles. In this fallacy, a person assumes that a series of causally unrelated events creates a causally linked pattern. Moreover, a person assumes that the longer the seeming pattern of events continues, the more likely it becomes that it will cease.[11] This fallacy supposedly caused a group of gamblers at a Monte Carlo casino to lose a great deal of money betting on roulette. According to the story, the roulette ball landed on black twenty-six times in a row.[12] During the game, gamblers assumed that the pattern would have to break soon and began betting huge amounts of money on red. But black kept returning and they lost a small fortune. Why? Because the odds of the ball landing on black each time is always 50 per cent regardless of previous outcomes. There is no causal connection between previous and future outcomes in this case.

You may not have much experience (yet?) with high-stakes gambling, but we also see this fallacy emerge when friends and family try to predict the biological sexes of their unborn children. If they have already had four boys, they often think the fifth child is more likely to be a girl. But, again, the odds are always only 50 per cent. If you already have nine boys, your tenth child is no more likely to be a girl than your first. Beware of the gambler's fallacy when you evaluate arguments critically. For example, someone may argue that because a certain politician or public figure has been found not guilty of criminal activity in the past, they are likely to be found guilty in the future, because the pattern has to break eventually. However, unless there is an actual causal connection between these verdicts, there is no "pattern" to break.

The opposite of the gambler's fallacy is the so-called *hot hand fallacy*. This fallacy also sees a series of causally unrelated events and regards them as a pattern. A person then assumes that the longer a sequence of events continues, the less likely the seeming pattern is to break.[13] In sports, we might talk about teams being on a winning streak. The longer they continue to win, the less likely we think they are to lose. Optimistic gamblers may think this way as well. Once they've started to win, they think it less likely that they will lose and may begin betting larger sums of money. The problem here is the same as in the gambler's fallacy. The events in the seeming patterns are not causally related, and so the outcome of preceding events does not make the succeeding events more or less likely. Again, be on the lookout for this fallacy in your sources. Arguments that the economy will continue to improve indefinitely – without reference to why this is the case – may be a version of the hot hand fallacy. Sometimes even professional historians and journalists fall into this fallacy when they assume that because certain contingent events like the expansion of social democracy and civil rights have happened in the past, they must continue to happen in the future. On the popular level, we see this in opinion pieces about this or that policy or events being on the "wrong side of history," as though historical events are necessarily and logically connected to one another and not contingent.

Informal Fallacies Related to Causation

Types of Causation

What do we mean when we say that one thing "caused" another thing to occur? Suppose one day I overslept and found myself late to my 8:00 a.m. class. Did oversleeping cause me to be late? What about my having scheduled a class at 8:00 a.m. in the first place? How about the fact that my alarm clock was broken? Can we call all of these "causes"? Obviously in one sense all three of these factors contributed to me being late and can therefore be considered "causes." At the same time, it should also be obvious that all three did not contribute to the effect, or end result, in the same way. This is because there are different types of causes, although we often obscure that fact by referring to them all as simply "causes." Historians and philosophers in particular love to think about causation. This trend goes all the way back to classical Greece and philosophers like Plato and Aristotle, who recognized that a thing can be responsible for something else occurring in a variety of different ways. As a result, Aristotle began to systematize different types of causation. Today, historiographers often cite "cause" or "causation" as one of the most important tools that help us interpret the past. Others tools could include change, context, contingency, and complexity. Together these form what historian John Fea calls the "five Cs of historical thinking."[14] Although each of the "Cs" is important, thinking about causation especially helps us to make sense of both how and why events happened the way they did. Moreover, it can also help us predict how events could unfold in the future.

Cause, then, is a powerful concept, but also one capable of being discussed in different ways. Although there are many different ways to subdivide causation, one way is to distinguish between indirect conditional necessary and direct primary agent causes. Both historical and contemporary events are exceedingly complex and based on many different variables. Having a precise way to talk about causation can help us refine our analytical abilities. Conditional necessary causes are necessary, but not sufficient, to explain an event. In other words, on the *condition* that such and such a thing happened, such and such was necessary in the sense, precisely, that if it were removed the thing would not have happened. What does this mean? To use our example above, in order to understand how I arrived late at class one day, I need to first explain that I had scheduled myself to teach an 8:00 a.m. class. Having a morning class was a necessary precondition to arriving late. Had it been an evening class, I could have overslept and it would not have mattered. However, I could obviously teach an 8:00 a.m. class and never arrive late. Thus, my decision to schedule an 8:00 a.m. class is necessary to explain what happened but not sufficient in and of itself. Note that necessary causes will always precede primary agent causes, which most directly cause an event to occur. You might want to think of necessary causes as background causes or preconditions. Remember, they are necessary for something to occur, but do not cause that thing to occur all by themselves.

Primary agent causes, on the other hand, are what we usually think of when we say something caused something else. These are immediate, direct causes. However, primary agent causes are always dependent on preexisting necessary causes. To return to our example, sleeping in most directly caused me to be tardy.[15] This was the primary agent cause. Note that the primary cause here depends on the necessary condition. If the class time was not 8:00 a.m., sleeping in would not have resulted in my being tardy.

Another type of cause is the contributory cause. If a cause is neither necessary nor sufficient but still increases the likelihood of an effect, then it's a contributory cause. Contributory causes can't cause or prevent the effect by themselves alone. Events can still occur without contributory causes being present. They can, however, make an event more or less likely. For example, having a broken alarm clock did not directly cause me to be late. Nor was it a necessary precondition. However, having a broken alarm clock increased the likelihood that I would at some point fail to wake up on my own and thereby oversleep since I had no mechanical failsafe.[16]

How can we know then if a cause is necessary, primary, or contributory? The first thing to consider is how far away the cause is from the effect. Is it an immediate cause? An intermediate one? Is it hundreds of years old? The most immediate causes are likely to be primary agent causes while more distant causes are likely to be necessary, or contributory, causes. However, the further in the past a cause is, the less relevant it is to the effect. We can also consider whether the cause appears to be a general cause or a more specific one. General causes are often necessary causes and form the context of primary agent causes. Finally, we can speculate about counterfactuals. What might have happened if something did not occur? If something could occur without a certain cause, then that cause is not a necessary cause. Conditional necessary causes are, after all, necessary.[17] In our example, it's not possible to be late for an 8:00 a.m. class if you don't have an 8:00 a.m. class.

To give another example, suppose I were to go hiking in the mountains, trip and fall walking along a perilous trail, and break my arm as a result. I've used this example in classes before and each time students get concerned and ask if I have really fallen off a mountain and broken my arm. For the record, I have not; this is a purely hypothetical scenario taken in part from the great historian Marc Bloch.[18] In any case, the mountain had to be there for me to break my arm when I tripped and fell off it. But, the mountain itself could be there without me breaking my arm. Therefore, the mountain existing is a conditional necessary cause of me breaking my arm. In this case, tripping and falling was the primary agent cause of me breaking my arm. Again, however, tripping and falling off the mountain is dependent on the mountain first existing. This confirms that tripping is the primary agent cause, since primary agent causes are dependent on preexisting necessary causes. Necessary causes, by contrast, are not dependent on primary agent causes. The mountain could still have been there without me tripping and falling off of it. There could also be contributory causes in this scenario. For example, my being rather clumsy increased my risk of tripping and falling. I could still trip, fall, and break an arm without being clumsy, but it certainly doesn't help. Neither does being clumsy in and of itself cause or prevent the accident from occurring.

Why have I bothered to go into such detail about causation? Because understanding and being able to talk and write clearly about cause will help us to become better communicators and readers. It will also enable us to become better interpreters of historical and current events. This in turn allows dialog partners to talk past each other less and get to where real disagreements – and maybe even agreements – may lie. For example, the writer of an op-ed piece on school shootings may argue that bullying, such as that suffered by the perpetrator the morning of the shooting, caused the mass murder to occur. Another may argue that inadequate gun control laws caused the shooting. There may be less disagreement here than it initially appears. The respective authors could be talking about cause in different ways. Whereas a bullying incident may have triggered the voluntary act of the shooter, making it an agent cause, the accessibility of guns may have been a necessary precondition. Writing more precisely about causation allows us to at least see where we still disagree and why.

Causation Exercise

Read the following paragraph on the origins of World War I (1914–18). On the basis of this paragraph, what would you say were the necessary cause or causes of the war? How about the primary agent cause? What about contributory causes? Why did you answer the way you did?

> Prior to the outbreak of World War I in 1914, Europe was a metaphorical battleground of competing nation-states and empires roughly divided between two main alliances and their clients. On the one hand was the Triple Entente, consisting of Britain, France, and Russia; on the other hand was the Triple Alliance of Germany, Austria-Hungary, and Italy. In 1914 all of the European states found themselves either attempting to harness or withstand the forces of nationalism, which had been sweeping through Europe since the mid-1800s. Nationalism proved to be a particularly destructive force in Austria-Hungary, since the dual monarchy encompassed many different nationalities who fervently desired nation-states of their own and sought to break away from the imperial government. Of these nationalities situated within Austrian territory, the Bosnian Serbs were perhaps the most insistent that they should be allowed independence. To achieve this goal, the Serbian nationalist group the Black Hand sought to assassinate the heir to the Austro-Hungarian throne,

Archduke Ferdinand, when he visited Sarajevo on June 28. June 28 was also a Serbian nationalist holiday known as St. Vitus's Day, but despite this, Austrian official Oskar Potiorek failed to make adequate security preparations. In any case, Serbian nationalist Gavrilo Princip assassinated Ferdinand and his wife before being captured. Austria blamed the independent state of Serbia, an ally of Russia, for the assassination and threatened to go to war. Austria's ally, Germany, agreed to support Austria's aggression. Russia supported Serbia, and France supported Russia. The alliance system pulled much of Europe into a larger conflagration in early August 1914.

Answers(?)

Historians have been debating the causes of World War I ever since it first broke out in 1914. Suffice it to say that there is no one correct set of answers to this exercise. Nevertheless, you could make a strong argument that the existence of two hostile alliances and an environment of militaristic nationalism constituted one necessary or background cause of the war. You could argue that the existence of pro-Serbian nationalist groups like the Black Hand constitutes an even more immediate necessary cause. In my World War I class, students generally argue that the assassination attempt constituted the literal smoking gun or primary agent cause of the war. Some students, however, mount effective arguments that it was not the assassination itself but the response on the part of Austria, Germany, Serbia, Russia, or France that constituted the true primary agent cause. One possible contributory cause here could be Oskar Potiorek's failure to make adequate preparations for the Archduke's visit to Sarajevo.

Correlation Is Not Causation: *Post Hoc, Ergo Propter Hoc*

Fallacies of Causation and Correlation:

- *post hoc, ergo propter hoc* (after this, therefore because of this)
- *cum hoc, ergo propter hoc* (with this, therefore because of this)

Now that we have our bearings with regard to causation in general, let's discuss some specific fallacies related to it. One of the most famous fallacies related to causation has another of those Latin names: *post hoc, ergo propter hoc*. Literally, the Latin phrase *post hoc, ergo propter hoc* means "after this, therefore because of this." This fallacy is also sometimes written as *post hoc, propter hoc* (after this, because of this). The *post hoc, ergo propter hoc* fallacy assumes that because event B happened after event A, event A must have caused event B. But remember that correlation is not the same as causation! To give an example, suppose you begin a diet consisting of nothing but pizza. A week later you get an A on your math test. You assume, therefore, that your all-pizza wonder diet transformed you into a mathematical genius. Wrong! Eating tons of pizza prior to earning an A on a math test does not necessarily mean that pizza *caused* you to get a good grade. You would need logic and evidence to prove the connection between the two. Otherwise, pizza merely correlated to a good grade; it did not cause it. The related fallacy of *cum hoc, ergo propter hoc* (with this, therefore because of this) also confuses correlation for a cause.[19] The *cum hoc* fallacy incorrectly assumes that because events A and B happened at the same time, event A must have caused event B. So perhaps you were eating pizza while taking that test you got an A on. Don't assume that the pizza fueled you to new heights of academic success, though. Unless you have invented some type of miraculous pizza, this is merely another instance of correlation rather than causation.

Reification: "Nationalism" Didn't Do That

Reification is another fallacy related to causation. It is a difficult sounding word, but it just means writing about an abstraction like it has a concrete existence that it doesn't really have. Generally, abstractions cannot be causal agents (things that make something happen by motion), so you can't talk about one like it is. For instance, "communism" or "imperialism" can't be agents, so you can't talk about them *doing* things. To do so would be to reify the abstract ideas, as though they are substantially existing and acting things in the world. So you should not write that "communism began the Bolshevik Revolution." Instead, write "V.I. Lenin, who was influenced by the ideology of socialism, began the Bolshevik Revolution."[20] Moreover, "Britain" or "America" can also function as abstractions if you write about them *doing* things. Technically, "Britain" didn't start the Industrial Revolution. Some British people did. In other example, "America" didn't invade Iraq in 2003. Rather, the American president and Congress authorized the United States Armed Forces to invade Iraq. History is driven by people and their ideas and actions, not by abstractions with no concrete historical reality.[21] Knowing that abstractions aren't real can help us figure out who or what is actually causing something to happen. And that knowledge can give us greater mastery over any given situation.

Fallacies of causation are among the most common in everyday conversation and writing. And it's easy to see why. There is the problem of what exactly is meant by "cause." The word itself can be used differently in different circumstances. And there is also the difficulty of discerning true causes from other factors. In other words, how do you know something is a cause and not a mere correlation? Moreover, we need to consider what exactly can function as a cause and why or why not. Sorting out these questions will help you think and express yourself more clearly. To practice thinking about causation, you'll find some exercises below.

Logical Fallacy Exercises

Now that you've learned about them, can you pick out the logical fallacies in the sentences below? Which logical fallacy or fallacies do you think each sentence contains? Why did you answer the way you did? You can identify the same fallacy more than once.

Fallacy Term Bank: *cum hoc, ergo propter hoc*; gambler's fallacy; hot hand fallacy; non sequitur; *post hoc, ergo propter hoc*; reification

1) Mr. Gorilla has been guilty of stealing bananas fifty times in the past. Therefore, he must necessarily have stolen bananas again.
2) Communism killed tens of millions of people.
3) The economy improved after the president was elected. Therefore, the president's election caused the economy to improve.

4) A country had a socialist economy when the economy collapsed. Therefore, socialism caused the economy to fail.
5) Climate change is occurring. Mr. Green acknowledges this. Therefore, Mr. Green should brush his teeth.
6) I got heads on twenty coin flips in a row, so future coin flips are therefore more likely to land on heads than tails.
7) Don't blame me! My anger broke the vase on the shelf!

Answers

1) This is the gambler's fallacy because there is no logical connection between having stolen the bananas in the past and stealing them again – besides gorillas' insatiable appetite for bananas, I suppose.
2) This is reification because "communism" is an abstract ideology. It did not directly kill anyone. People inspired by communism did.
3) This is the *post hoc, ergo propter hoc* (after this, therefore because of this) fallacy because it assumes that since the economy improved *after* the president was elected, it improved *because* the president was elected. Logically there could be other causes.
4) This is the *cum hoc, ergo propter hoc* (with this, therefore because of this) fallacy because it assumes that since the economy was failing *while* a socialist government held power, the socialist government *caused* the economy to fail. Logically, there could be other causes. Strictly speaking, this includes reification, since "socialism" as an abstract idea in and of itself lacks causative power. Only humans influenced by socialism and enacting socialist policies influenced the economy.
5) This is a non sequitur. Mr. Green brushing his teeth has no connection to climate change occurring or to Mr. Green acknowledging that fact. The conclusion here does not follow from the premises.
6) This is the hot hand fallacy because the outcome of each coin flip is unrelated to previous flips and therefore odds of heads is always only 50 per cent.
7) This is reification since "anger" is an abstraction. Your anger didn't break the vase. You did!

CHAPTER 7

FALLACIES OF NARRATION, GENERALIZATION, AND EVIDENCE

Fallacies of Narration

Anachronism: Abraham Lincoln Says Not to Believe Everything on the Internet

Since discussing causation involves narrating something, we now come to fallacies of narration. One of the most well known of these is the infamous anachronism. This occurs when something appears in a narration outside of the time or place in which it belongs. Another way of looking at anachronisms is that they put things from different periods or places together in impossible ways. You might encounter anachronisms when you watch a period drama and complain that the costuming was not accurate because George Washington wore a leisure suit popular in the 1970s. Another example that you may have seen floating around social media is a satirical meme featuring a painting of Abraham Lincoln, who lived between 1809 and 1865, and a quotation reading "The trouble with quotes on the internet is that it's difficult to discern whether or not they are genuine." Unless Abraham Lincoln was immortal or a time-traveler, he had no knowledge of the internet. Therefore, he certainly couldn't have had trouble determining the credibility of online sources. A more academic example would be arguing that the English peasant uprising of 1381 was a working-class revolution. Marxist historiography notwithstanding, this is anachronistic since "class," at least in the modern sense of the word, did not come into existence until the Industrial Revolution in the late eighteenth and nineteenth centuries.[1]

The Twin Fallacies of Appeal to Progress and Tradition

Another fallacy of narration is the *appeal to progress or novelty*. Not surprisingly, this fallacy is common among those with a progressive worldview. In general, progressives see change or reform as good. Therefore, the temptation for progressives is to argue that because something is new, it is good. So, for example, allowing women into combat positions in the US Armed Forces is a wise policy because it is a reform. Progressives may also interpret any change to society as automatically for the best without pausing for further reflection. Because most modern Westerners have a reflexively progressive view of history, derived from thinkers such as Charles Darwin and Karl Marx, there is a tendency to deem any major reforms or changes as being on the "right side of history," as though history – reified – picked sides.

On the other side of the appeal to progress, however, is the *appeal to tradition*, which we will discuss again later in its guise as an *appeal to irrelevant authority*. If political progressives are tempted to see change as automatically good, then conservatives are more likely to see something as good because it is old or traditional. After all, conservatives are attempting to conserve some already existing thing of value. Not surprisingly then, when conservatives want to argue that something is good, they may attempt to show that it is traditional or part of the status quo. In arguing that the Roman Catholic Church is a valuable institution in spite of recent sexual abuse scandals, they may point out that it is traditional. Another fallacy somewhat related to the appeal to tradition is what a delightful little book entitled *Logical Fallacy Monsters* calls the *nirvana fallacy*.[2] Those propagating this fallacy hold that if something cannot be done absolutely perfectly, it should not be attempted at all. But nothing can be done perfectly. Therefore, the practical result of this fallacy is that we should always maintain the traditional status quo. An example of this might be someone arguing that because it's impossible to undo all of the damage caused to the environment by industrialization, we shouldn't even try. Or that because it's unrealistic to outlaw all abortion procedures, none should be outlawed.

Of course, the appeal to tradition and the appeal to progress are both fallacies. A policy or belief or institution is not necessarily good or bad because it is new or because it is old. While it is certainly defensible to hold that a progressive teleological view of history necessitates giving reform the benefit of the doubt, or that a belief that the longevity of institutions gives evidence of their functionality and therefore it is imprudent to tinker with them, we should nevertheless also rationally judge each instance on its own merits.

Fallacies of Generalization: Not All Democrats Are Socialists

Hasty Generalizations

Narration lends itself to generalization. As a result, there are numerous fallacies of generalization. These fallacies occur when someone uses a single piece of evidence (or an unrepresentative sample) and then generalizes to make an argument about a whole class of things or events. The *fallacy of generalization* is related to statistical sampling fallacies, which generalize based on samples that are too small to be properly representative.[3] Generalizations usually appear in specific forms, like hasty or sweeping generalizations, to which we will return below.[4] Hasty generalizations, for example, rely on an inadequate sample size. For example, if a person saw only three cats, which all happened to be black, and then concluded that all cats are therefore black, he made a hasty generalization. The related *fallacy of the lonely* fact makes a generalization on the basis of a single lonely fact.[5] When reading scholarly material, you should also be on the lookout for arguments that apply findings beyond their original scope.[6] This is yet another type of inappropriate generalization.

Another of these hasty generalizations is *tokenism*. This fallacy puts forward a single instance, or token, of something and then either implicitly or explicitly encourages you to generalize on the basis of that instance. But why would someone want to encourage others to make an erroneous generalization? Often times an organization or person wants to appear more tolerant, diverse, or devoted to equality than they really are.[7] For example, a college at which 95 per cent of the student body is white may send out marketing materials showing a group of ten students. Of these ten, four are people of color. That is 40 per cent of the total! In this case, the students of color in the promotional photo may serve as tokens to give the impression that the school is more racially diverse than it actually is. The marketing material might cause prospective students to assume that in an average group of ten students, four are nonwhite. And yet, this would be an erroneous generalization. We see tokenism frequently in the media as well. A newspaper known to be left leaning may argue that it does not have a liberal bias. Why? Because it employs one token conservative opinion writer.

Slippery Slope

Another type of generalization is the slippery slope argument. The slippery slope presupposes that if one thing happens, then it will lead to a chain of events, like dominos, and eventually bring about a final – usually very bad – result. For example, if Republicans eliminate federal funding to Planned Parenthood, America will become a theocracy. If LGBTQ+ people can marry, the country will decline into moral and sexual anarchy. As you can see, the slippery slope argument often works in concert with appeals to fear. Of course, there *may* be a logical causal connection between eliminating federal funding and theocratic tyranny, or between same-sex marriage and moral and sexual anarchy. But these connections would need to be established through an explanation of the relevant evidence.

Fallacies of Composition and Division

You've probably already heard of slippery slope arguments, but other less well-known fallacies of generalization also exist. These include the fallacies of composition and division. The *fallacy of composition* occurs when you take the properties of a single individual or thing in a group and then assign those properties to the group as a whole.[8] This can become a type of hasty generalization when the individual, group, or characteristic functions as a whole sample. For example, I might say that the window is glass, therefore the house is glass. The *fallacy of division*, on the other hand, occurs when you apply the aggregate characteristics of a group to individuals within the group. This fallacy often leads to stereotyping.

Defining through common characteristics is a pitfall somewhat similar to the fallacies of division and composition in that they involve the relationship between the characteristics of a group and individuals. In the *common characteristics fallacy*, however, you suppose that because a person has certain characteristics in common with a group, he must be a member of that group.[9] But this is not necessarily the case. You might assume that because Beth supports abortion rights she is a member of the Democratic Party, which also supports abortion rights. However, Beth could just as easily be a pro-choice member of the Republican Party.

Oversimplification: Do Not Keep It Simple, Stupid

We oversimplify when we fail to identify all relevant factors in a given situation. In the field of history, this fallacy often refers to oversimplifying causation. Oversimplification more broadly becomes the *fallacy of the single cause* when we argue that only one thing is the cause of something when in fact many things are. Remember that events in the real world generally have multiple causes.[10] Oversimplification is related to the *reductive fallacy*, which "reduces complexity to simplicity, or diversity to uniformity, in causal explanations."[11] Historian John Lewis Gaddis calls on us to reject the "doctrine of immaculate causation, which seems to be implied in the idea that one can identify, without reference to all that has preceded it, such a thing as an independent variable. Causes always have antecedents. We may rank their relative significance, but we'd think it irresponsible to seek to isolate – or 'tease out' – single causes for complex events."[12] We see oversimplification frequently in contemporary political and economic debates. For example, a person may argue that the American economy is declining relative to other economies because of the North American Free Trade Agreement. But surely it is an oversimplification to say that such a complex phenomenon as the entire domestic economy is determined entirely on the basis of a single international trade agreement, important though it may be.

Interestingly, our modern penchant to explain things in terms of conspiracy theories is a version of oversimplification. We live in a complex globalized world, and seemingly mysterious invisible forces thousands of miles away impact our socioeconomic lives all the time. How can we explain the upheaval caused in our lives by a thousand impersonal variables that may determine our employment status or form of government? But what if there was a single personal root cause creating and manipulating these insidious forces? Wouldn't that make problems easier to understand and solve? By eliminating or reforming the root cause, you could potentially fix everything. This thinking forms the basis of conspiracy theories. Although what believers consider the "root cause" may differ – and has included everything from Freemasons to the deep state to a vast criminal conspiracy revealed by an anonymous government official known only as Q – the fallacious thinking remains the same: that we can explain complex world events through reference to a single conspiracy or conspiratorial actors. This line of thinking is appealing because simple problems are easier to solve than complex ones. It's easier to bring down a criminal conspiracy than it is to resolve structural inequalities and other socioeconomic problems. Of course, this is not to say that no conspiracies have ever existed, merely that inventing them is one means of oversimplification.

Other types of oversimplification are stereotyping and sloganeering. Both individuals and groups can be stereotyped.[13] When groups are stereotyped, characteristics of individuals within a larger group are exaggerated and generalized to apply to the group as a whole. For example, Republicans are wealthy and old, and Democrats are less well-to-do and young. The visual version of stereotyping is caricature, wherein specific individual features are exaggerated for effect, be it humor or something more insidious. The use of slogans also helps simplify an argument. Is there any need to debate the merits or demerits of health-care reform when one side is clearly offering "Hope and Change"? Why wade into the murky waters of immigration policy when we can simply "Make America Great Again"?

Sweeping Generalizations

Moving away from derivatives of the hasty generalization, sweeping generalizations apply a sound generalization to instances that should be exceptions. In *Thinking Critically*, philosopher John Chaffee gives this example: "Vigorous exercise contributes to overall good health. Therefore vigorous exercise should be practiced by recent heart attack victims."[14] Although "vigorous exercise contributes to overall good health" is not a hasty generalization – the conclusion was made on the basis of a representative sample – recent heart attack victims ought to be an exception to the generalization. Please do not train for triathlons if you are recovering from quadruple bypass surgery! To give another example, generally you should get plenty of sleep and not stay up too late. However, if you have procrastinated on writing a term paper that is due the next day, this generalization does not hold. Applying it will probably not impress your professor, who will note that you've really made a sweeping generalization.

Fallacies of Choice: Pick One or the Other

Another common fallacy related to generalization is the *false dilemma*. This is a fallacy of choice and you may hear it also referred to as the *either-or fallacy*. In this fallacy, you find yourself confronted with only two incompatible take-it-all-or-leave-it options. You then feel compelled to choose between the two positions. In other words, you need to pick either option A in its entirety or option B. If you don't want option A, then you'll need to pick option B. Often, one of the two options will be so undesirable that the listener will feel forced into selecting the less abhorrent of the two options, even if it seems less than ideal. Sometimes this becomes a lesser-of-two-evils argument when we are arguing with ourselves over a difficult decision. Perhaps neither option is appealing. Which to pick? The lesser of the two evils. In any case, although sometimes there may really be only two choices, and we are genuinely faced with a situation of being forced to pick all of A or all of B, things are generally less black and white. In fact, this fallacy is also sometimes referred to as the *black-and-white fallacy*.[15] In reality, we almost always have more than two radically incompatible, all-or-nothing options. For example, you could choose to support aspects of option A *and* aspects of option B. To say that you *must* pick all of A or all of B is usually a false dilemma.

We see this informal fallacy pop up in many different places. For example, advertisers might argue that if you want clean teeth you must use Mouthwash A every day, otherwise your teeth will rot out of your mouth. In truth, you could also brush your teeth or use a different mouthwash and maintain shiny white teeth without recourse to Mouthwash A. Setting aside oral hygiene, this fallacy frequently shows up in politics. In America's two-party system, many voters may be dissatisfied with the candidates of both major parties but nevertheless receive the message that these are the only two choices and therefore they *must* pick one and support *all* of that candidate's positions. Now, there may be good political reasons for voting for one or the other main party candidates as a lesser of two evils, but there is no logical reason why you necessarily have to do so. In the 2020 US presidential election, I noticed this fallacy on display quite a bit. Friends argued either that they *had* to vote for Donald Trump because otherwise they would be voting for the collapse of religious liberty protections or that they *had* to vote for Joe Biden because otherwise they would be voting for gender and sexual minorities to lose civil rights. Again (at least logically speaking), these arguments are false dilemmas because things are not so black and white in reality. It was logically possible to support protection for religious liberty without also voting for Trump. Likewise, it was logically possible to support safeguarding the civil rights of gender and sexual minority groups without voting for Biden.

Fallacies of Evidence

Fallacies Related to "Factual Verification"

Moving on from generalizations, we come to fallacies of evidence, including what historical logician David Hackett Fischer calls fallacies of "factual verification."[16] What happens when evidence doesn't support an argument? The *fallacy of the negative proof* occurs when an arguer attempts to prove an argument using only negative evidence. As Fischer puts it, the fallacy of the negative proof "occurs whenever a historian declares that 'there is no evidence that X is the case,' and then proceeds to affirm or assume that not-X is the case."[17] Remember that an argument must be supported with *positive* proof. In order to do this, an arguer must explain the connection between the thesis being proven and the evidence being used. The arguer must also use the best possible relevant positive evidence. This is because "the burden of proof, for any ... assertion, always rests upon its author."[18] But remember, an argument cannot be more precise or specific than what the evidence allows. When I wrote this in early 2019, special prosecutor Robert Mueller was still leading an investigation into possible Russian interference in the 2016 American presidential election. As news relating to the investigation continually hit the electronic and print headlines, the fallacy of the negative proof afflicted both supporters and opponents of President Trump. Democratic opponents argued that collusion between Trump and Russia has not been disproven (yet) and so, therefore, it happened. Republican supporters, on the other hand, argued that since there was no evidence (yet) of Russian collusion, it did not happen. As we now know, though, you cannot prove an argument with an absence of evidence.

Other related fallacies of evidence are the fallacies of the unknowable fact and the irrelevant proof. In the *fallacy of the unknowable fact*, we cannot know one of the premises with certainty.[19] This renders the argument purely speculative. For example, someone might argue that if there had been stricter gun laws, a certain mass shooting wouldn't have happened. Or someone else might argue that if the shooter had had a father figure in his life, he wouldn't have killed so many people.

The *fallacy of the irrelevant proof*, on the other hand, occurs when someone asks one question and then winds up answering a different one.[20] A variant of this fallacy can also occur when someone makes an argument of some kind but then provides evidence that is irrelevant to the original claim. For example, a writer might argue that deforestation in South America is a serious global threat because of its impact on climate change. But then as evidence the writer cites baseball statistics. Always make sure that evidence is relevant to and supports claims.

One type of evidence that especially lends itself to misuse is numbers. This is perhaps because people tend to have a hard time understanding statistics and as a result are more likely to believe anecdotal evidence, which is itself the *anecdotal fallacy*.[21] The result of all this is that one can commit fallacy via statistics in innumerable ways, many of which overlap with fallacies of generalization. Robert Gula does a fine job of laying them out in his book *Nonsense*.[22] Some of the most common statistical fallacies involve averages. Types of averages include the median and the mode. The median orders a group of numbers in sequence and then selects the middle number. The mode average is the most frequently appearing number. Perhaps the most commonly used type of average, however, is the mean average. As you may recall from high school math, mean averages simply calculate a sum and then divide by the number of figures.

To give one example, the National Hot Dog and Sausage Council calculates that Americans eat twenty billion hot dogs each year.[23] A hot dog lover could divide those twenty billion hot dogs by the total American population and then argue that the average American eats seventy hot dogs per year. Therefore, hot dogs deserve more respect. Despite your friend's mathematical chops, you should be justifiably skeptical that the average American actually eats seventy hot dogs per year. Remember that when someone tells you a number is an average, that number could be saying a variety of different things. The figure of seventy hot dogs per person is the mean average, which is usually what someone intends when citing an average. With the mean average, though, perhaps no one real person is actually eating seventy hot dogs per year. Rabid hot dog fanatics may be eating hundreds in stadiums across the country, while other Americans are not eating any. The reality, then, is that some Americans, like my toddler, eat many more than seventy hot dogs and some eat far fewer. As a result, the mean average may not give enough information to support an argument.

Other fallacies of quantification often occur because of insufficient sample sizes. For example, you could argue that 75 per cent of your sample size supports the Democratic candidate for mayor of a large city. Therefore, the Democratic candidate is likely to win. You are shocked when the Republican candidate wins! The problem? You only surveyed four people. Of those four, three supported the Democratic candidate, which gave you the 75 per cent figure. Obviously four is an insufficient sample size if you want to predict the outcome of an election involving perhaps hundreds of thousands of voters. Unscrupulous advertisers or debaters can intentionally manipulate the sample size or the types of people sampled to yield their desired results. For example, if you wanted to gauge the level of enthusiasm for a new movie in your hometown, surveying only people lined up to see the movie on opening night would not provide a representative sample. People camped out in tents for days to see the latest installment of a sci-fi epic are likely to have a much higher level of enthusiasm than the general population.[24] We see that improper use of evidence could lead to faulty generalizations – the entire city is full of sci-fi lovers – and that these generalizations could then be used to craft an inaccurate narrative.

Like the fallacies of causation we examined in the last chapter, fallacies of narrative, generalization, and evidence are quite common. This is especially true recently as a result of the 2020 novel coronavirus pandemic. Individuals latch onto a single piece of (perhaps dubious) information about the virus and then fall into error as a result of generalizing. Given the mountain of data related to COVID-19 cases and deaths, it's also not surprising that statistical fallacies have become commonplace. Luckily, the ability to spot fallacies such as the ones we've seen above can help you identity these instances of the misuse of evidence, defective generalizations, and mistaken narratives.

Logical Fallacy Exercises

Now that you've learned about them, can you pick out the logical fallacies in the sentences below? Which logical fallacy or fallacies do you think each sentence contains? Why did you answer the way you did? You can pick the same fallacy more than once.

Fallacy Term Bank: anachronism, appeal to tradition, common characteristics, false dilemma, negative proof, oversimplification, slippery slope, stereotype, unknowable fact

1) There is no evidence of sentient life on other planets. Therefore, it does not exist.
2) Beth is a feminist and Democrat. Therefore, she must be pro-choice.
3) If America adopts a single-payer health-care system, we will become a communist country.
4) Supporters of the Republican presidential candidate are all racist hillbillies.
5) I remember cruising around town in my electric car with my smartphone back in the 1980s. It was so much fun!
6) Supporters of the Democratic presidential candidate are all lazy communists.
7) If you want to improve access to health care in America, you must support a single-payer system.
8) Cow farts produce methane, which contributes to global warming. We can reduce the cause of climate change to cow farts. Therefore, we need to kill off all the cows to save the earth.
9) If only the environmentalist Al Gore had become US president in 2001, the polar ice caps would not be melting now.
10) The British monarchy is a wonderful institution because it is so old and traditional. We should never change it.

Answers
1) This is the fallacy of the negative proof. Just because there is no evidence of sentient life, it does not logically follow that there is no sentient life on other planets.
2) This is the fallacy of common characteristics. Just because many supporters of abortion rights have the additional characteristics of also being feminists and Democrats doesn't mean that Beth as an individual has those characteristics. She could be a pro-life feminist Republican.

3) This is the slippery slope fallacy. It assumes that once the first thing happens, it will inevitably lead to a chain of events that will end in communism.

4) This statement stereotypes supporters of the Republican presidential candidate.

5) In addition to illustrating my poor memory, this is an anachronism because electric cars and smartphones did not exist in the 1980s.

6) This statement stereotypes supporters of the Democratic presidential candidate.

7) This is a false dilemma because it is possible that there are other ways to improve access to health care in America besides a single-payer system.

8) This is the fallacy of oversimplification. Other factors besides cattle contribute to climate change, and solutions need to consider many other relevant factors.

9) This is the fallacy of the unknowable fact. We can never know what would have happened if Al Gore had become president because it did not, in fact, happen.

10) This is an appeal to tradition because age functions as the primary reason for attributing value to the monarchy.

CHAPTER 8

FALLACIES OF DIVERSION

Fallacies of Diversion: Don't Look Here! Look Over There!

Fallacies of Intrusion

Let's wrap up our tour of fallacies with some of the most common types of informal fallacies: *fallacies of diversion*. These fallacies try to divert your attention away from the actual argument and relevant evidence in order to score points. First, we'll look at some diversionary fallacies of intrusion.[1] One of the most obvious fallacies of diversion is *special pleading*. When an arguer is engaging in special pleading, he may either ignore the counterargument against his position altogether or even admit that his own argument actually is weak. Nevertheless, the special pleader thinks that there should be, for some reason, a special exception for his case. Not only that, but the arguer fails to explain *why* a special exception should apply.[2] For example, arguing that federal government policy should be driven by scientific consensus, but not in the case of climate change, could be a case of special pleading. However, not all instances of special pleading constitute informal fallacies. There really may be a reason to make exceptions in certain cases. In the above instance, perhaps the arguer believes the inability to reach international consensus on climate policy invalidates the need to act at the national level based on scientific consensus. The key here is to explain *why* an exception should apply. Otherwise, you've stumbled into or uncovered an informal logical fallacy.

Red Herring

We've probably all heard of the infamous *red herring fallacy*, but you may not know the origins of its name. You probably do know, however, that in the past detectives used hound dogs to sniff out their prey. If you were a criminal fleeing dogged hounds – pun intended – one tactic was supposedly to distract your four-legged pursuers by dragging a herring across the path. The new fishy scent sent the hounds off in a different direction while you escaped.[3] The mental image of criminals on the lamb with a pocketful of rotting herring amuses me, so I hope this is a true story. In any case, in informal logic, red herring fallacies occur when an arguer metaphorically drags a stinky dead fish across the logical path. This tactic results in the opponent becoming distracted and eventually sidetracked away from the content of the original argument. Basically, red herrings are classic fallacies of diversion. And given that there are so many different ways to distract an opponent, diversionary fallacies exist in a vast array. For example, there is the well-known *"two wrongs make a right" fallacy*.

Two Wrongs Make a Right

If you have a sibling, you are probably quite familiar with this fallacy. As children, your brother may have punched you in the arm. You responded by punching your brother in the leg. Your mother asked you why you punched little Jimmy. You said that he punched you first. And she responded by saying that "two wrongs don't make a right" and sending you both off to time-out. Whether or not you knew it at the time, your mother was catching you in an informal fallacy. Wasn't she clever! Even though this fallacy is fairly easy to spot once you are looking, it is very common indeed, especially in contemporary political discourse. Whole political strategies are based around the argument that although my candidate may have done a bad thing, your candidate also did a bad thing. Therefore, we can excuse my candidate. Of course, two wrongs do not cancel each other out. And they certainly do not make one right, as your mother can almost certainly tell you.

The related *tu quoque*, or "you too," *fallacy* occurs when you accuse someone of being a hypocrite. The assumption is that the other person's hypocrisy excuses your own behavior. In a sense, this is another, more specific, version of the "two wrongs make a right" argument. For example, suppose you discover that a friend has been gossiping about you. You confront her about this. But rather than directly address the issue at hand, she replies that it shouldn't matter because you gossip as well! Now, you may well be a gossip, but whether you are or aren't is irrelevant in this case and simply distracts from your initial concerns. Robert Gula notes that the *tu quoque* fallacy is sometimes called the *"shifting the blame" fallacy* since the arguer attempts to distract by shifting the blame off himself and onto someone else.[4]

Genetic Fallacy: Just Because Trump or Clinton Said It Doesn't Make It Wrong

Another diversionary tactic is the *genetic fallacy*. This fallacy is "the error of allowing the origins of something to determine its current nature or meaning."[5] Consequently, attention moves away from the content of an argument and toward its origins. Suppose you strongly dislike former US President Donald Trump. Despite this fact, just because Trump says something doesn't necessarily mean it's not also true. Do not assume that the dodgy origins of something always make it wrong or false.[6] On the other hand, neither do the origins of something automatically make it correct or true. Just because a very smart and respected person like physicist Neil deGrasse Tyson or Fred Rogers said something doesn't make it true. The only way to determine whether a statement is true or false is through critical investigation. This is where you would need to employ all the skills you learned in the preceding chapters.

Appeal to Irrelevant Authority

Appealing to an irrelevant authority can also distract a reader from the argument itself. In the appeal to authority (*argumentum ad verecundiam*) an arguer cites some apparent authority figure to add additional heft to an argument. Obviously, it *is* important to cite sources. This is how you deploy evidence to support your argument. And these sources must be authoritative, as we discussed above. However, citing authoritative sources is not the problem here. Rather, a fallacy occurs when an arguer cites an *irrelevant* authority. As we noted in a previous chapter, just having a terminal degree does not qualify someone to opine on any subject matter. Remember that a PhD in biology does not make someone an authority on theology, and Hollywood celebrity status does not make someone an expert in international affairs. Even if a person's credential *seems* to be in the relevant area, dig deeper. As we have seen, a person with a PhD in biology, broadly speaking, has some authority to speak on the topic of vaccinations. However, a specialty in ecology is less relevant to the topic of vaccinations than other biological specialties. Ecologists may know a lot about ecosystems but less about whether or not to vaccinate your child. Apply the CRAAP test and check credentials, because citing or quoting irrelevant authorities does not strengthen an argument.

Much like ice cream, but less delicious, these fallacious appeals to authority come in different flavors. There is the *appeal to past authorities*. This sometimes occurs when someone picks a famous (or infamous) thinker or politician and cherry-picks a quotation to support his or her argument. Long-dead Greek philosophers are popular choices, as are the American Founding Fathers.[7] This informal fallacy is very common in student papers precisely because it is so easy to accomplish and therefore so tempting. Writing a research paper? Just Google "Founding Fathers quotations." By clicking on the first search result (in October 2020 this was a website called Founding Fathers Quotes: Our Favorite Quotes from America's Courageous Revolutionaries) we come to a site with dozens of quotations you could use to add luster to your writing.[8] The first problem here is that adding a quotation without explaining its context does not provide evidence of anything. Quotations from past authorities are only useful as evidence if you can first adequately explain their original context and why they are relevant to your topic. Otherwise, you may fall into an anachronism. Secondly, in this specific case, you should note that the domain of this website of quotes by Founding Fathers is hosted by Ammo. com, which is actually designed primarily to sell discount ammunition online. As a result, the quotations that the website designers selected are all biased toward an interpretation of the Second Amendment that favors the ready availability of a wide variety of guns and ammunition. This means that the quotations available are both out of context and the product of a particular selection bias.

Another type of appeal to authority that you may encounter on websites and especially in advertisements is the vague appeal to authority.[9] Here an arguer may claim that scientific authorities support changes to policies regarding carbon emissions. But who are these "scientific authorities"? It's a vague claim. Perhaps these scientists are relevant authorities, but you have no way of knowing without first investigating their identities. Another vague appeal to authority is the *sacred cow*. Here the arguer is appealing not to a vague group of people but rather to a vague ideal that could mean different things to different people. Despite being vague, however, the sacred cow derives its holiness from the fact that regardless of how it is defined, nearly everyone reveres it. In America, sacred cows include equality, democracy, liberty, and patriotism.[10] These concepts are as American as mom and apple pie, as they say. As a result, if an arguer claims that his argument supports one of these sacred cows it becomes extremely difficult to launch an effective rebuttal. Say your opponent claims his argument defends liberty. Suddenly, if you attack your opponent's argument you are attacking the sacred cow of liberty itself. And who would dare defile Lady Liberty? Shame! Again, the problem with this fallacy is that creating a sacred cow diverts attention away from evidence and logic. Instead, the arguer forces his opponent into the uncomfortable position of defending himself against the charge of hating freedom, equality, or the like. We can see an example of the sacred cow fallacy when an arguer claims, for example, that various affirmative action policies are essential to ensure equality. First, one might question what exactly "equality" means in this context. Second, since no one wants to attack the vaguely defined sacred cow of equality, the opponent of these policies might find herself immediately on the defensive.

Straw Man: Republicans Hate Poor People and Democrats Hate America

Claiming that your opponent is violating a sacred cow can shift into a *straw man fallacy*, which distracts from the argument by making an opponent appear extra ignorant, or worse. This infamous fallacy occurs when you attribute certain views to your opponents but they don't actually hold those views. As a result, you have distracted your opponent from the actual issue since she is instead forced to defend or explain away a position she does not really hold. For example: "My opponents, the Republicans, want to make poor people even poorer.

This means their economic policies are wrong because we should want to make the poor wealthier." This is a straw man argument because, despite whatever other beliefs they may have, Republicans do not, in fact, want to make poor people even poorer. Straw man arguments tend to oversimplify or misrepresent another argument in order to make it easier to attack. When responding to an argument, you need to always argue against an accurate presentation of your opponent's position.[11] This means you'll also need to develop reading and listening skills in addition to empathy so you can put yourself in another person's shoes and understand her arguments, as is required by the principle of charity.

Yet another version of the straw man fallacy is *attacking the alternative*. In this fallacy, an arguer might realize that his own position is weak or he is unable to defend it for some reason. Therefore, rather than defend his own position from an opponent's arguments, he attacks a supposedly necessary alternative to his position.[12] This may seem a little abstract, but look at this example. Suppose that one person wants to argue in favor of increased gun control. However, he is having a difficult time arguing in favor of his position or defending it against the attacks of his adversary. Therefore, he instead decides to attack an alternative. He may say, "How can you oppose gun control? If we don't have gun control, then we'll need to close schools altogether to ensure the safety of children and then no one will get educated. Therefore, we obviously need to pass more gun control legislation." Notice that the arguer did not actually address the reasons why his opponent was opposed to gun control. Instead, he attacked a hypothetical – and obviously unacceptable – alternative straw man scenario.

Scapegoating

Another type of diversionary fallacy you've probably heard of is *scapegoating*. The term "scapegoat" comes from an Old Testament Jewish ritual prescribed for the Day of Atonement. The author of the book of Leviticus writes that the Jewish high priest "shall lay both his hands on the head of the live goat, and confess over it all the iniquities of the people of Israel, and all their transgressions, all their sins. And he shall put them on the head of the goat and send it away into the wilderness by the hand of a man who is in readiness."[13] In other words, the community used the expulsion of an innocent sacrificial goat to help resolve the problem of sin. Today we scapegoat an individual person or a group when we blame them for some problem without justification or evidence. Scapegoating is easy because the victimized group is usually an unpopular minority. Therefore, others in the majority are unlikely to demand evidence that actually proves the condemned group is to blame. Scapegoating is a diversionary fallacy because rather than seeking to resolve a problem or issue, it just shifts the blame.

Historically, this fallacy has had utterly horrific consequences. The example that perhaps springs most readily to mind is the way Nazis scapegoated Jews for Germany's loss in World War I and interwar socioeconomic troubles. To simplify, Nazi ideologues argued that since Jews were to blame for Germany's problems (a claim that was obviously false), those problems could be solved via genocide. The Second World War gave the Nazi government the opportunity to carry out their plans, which resulted in the tragic deaths of at least six million Jews. Sadly, the Holocaust was not the first or last time scapegoating resulted in genocide. Here's a lesser known, earlier example. As the First World War raged in 1915, the Turkish government feared its minority Armenian population was undermining the war effort. In an effort to prevent this, the Turkish government sought to expel or eliminate the Armenian population, which resulted in the deaths of at least one million innocent subjects of the Turkish Ottoman Empire. Given scapegoating's track record of inflicting unparalleled real-world suffering, this is a fallacy you should always avoid.

Fallacies Attacking the Arguer: Abusive ad Hominem

Ad hominem (to the person) arguments distract by directing attention away from logic and evidence and instead focusing it on the person making the argument. As is the case with many informal fallacies, ad hominem fallacies come in many flavors. Perhaps the most popular is the *abusive ad hominem*, which attacks the person rather than engaging the content of the argument itself. I have no doubt you are familiar with this style of argumentation. For example, rather than attempt to rebut my argument, someone may just claim, "Dr. Kilcrease is a jerk. Therefore she's wrong." Now, it may well be true that Dr. Kilcrease is, in fact, a jerk. This, however, does not determine whether or not my argument is sound. Sadly, we see the abusive ad hominem rear its ugly head in political discourse quite frequently. Fiscal conservatives are greedy and selfish, social liberals are whiny "snowflakes," and so on; therefore, we can discount all they say. This is rubbish. The good news is that these are some of the easiest of all logical fallacies to spot and avoid. If an arguer is attacking his opponent instead of the content of the argument itself, you've got an ad hominem on your hands.

A relatively common specific form of this fallacy is the *circumstantial ad hominem*. This is a slightly more subtle form of the abusive ad hominem argument. Here the attacker attempts to discredit an arguer's position by attacking not the arguer herself but her motives.[14] For example, someone could argue that you only support government subsidies for sustainable energy because you own a company that makes solar panels. Another type of ad hominem attack is *guilt by association*. In this fallacy, the opponent ignores the actual argument and instead attacks the arguer based on her friends, family, or colleagues. For example, one might argue that we should not listen to anything Susy has to say because several of her friends are socialists. Or we should not engage with Joe's argument because he was raised by a family of Traditionalist Catholics. In each case, an arguer attempts to distract you from the real content of the argument by focusing your attention on real or imagined defects in his opponent.

All these ad hominem arguments contribute to a phenomenon called "poisoning the well." British theologian John Henry Newman first deployed the term in his autobiographical *Apologia Pro Vita Sua* (1864), which defended his decision to convert to Roman Catholicism. The term itself harkens back to the practice of external enemy armies or internal subversives poisoning city wells to destroy defenses from within. Rhetorical poisoning occurs when one arguer attacks the other in such a way that readers or listeners will automatically disagree with anything the poisoning victim says. This renders further argumentation impossible.[15] As a result, the defenses collapse and the poisoner wins the argument by default. This, however, is not a very honorable way to win either a war or an argument. Since the ability to maintain open dialog is an important component of critical thinking, don't be diverted by ad hominem arguments.

Appeals to Emotion

Another of the most effective ways to divert attention away from the logic of an argument is by appealing to emotion. Once we feel sufficiently sad, angry, or excited, it's difficult to think rationally about evidence and argumentation. This is why stories that evoke emotions (like clickbait) are shared more on social media than those that don't.[16] And this resulting inability to think rationally may be exactly what the arguer wants. Common variants of the appeal to emotion include the appeal to pity, or *argumentum ad misericordiam*. To my mind, the best example of this comes from the classic American Society for the Prevention of Cruelty to Animals (ASPCA) fund-raising commercial. The commercial, which first aired in 2007, featured images of abused animals set to singer Sarah McLachlan's song "Angel." The commercial, which neither I nor Sarah McLachlan are able to bear watching to this day, apparently moved so many Americans to salty tears of pity that it raised the ASPCA $30 million within two years.[17] Related to the appeal to pity is the appeal to guilt, which aims to make you feel guilty for not acquiescing to the demands of the arguer. As the ASPCA argues, "we are their [the animals'] voice."[18] The implication, of course, is that failing to donate to the ASPCA is a dereliction of duty to abused animals.

In addition to stirring up pity and guilt, arguers also try to manipulate opponents by creating fear. This fallacy is known as the *appeal to fear*, or *argumentum ad metum*. In this argument's classic form, an arguer claims that if a person does A, then B will happen. Or, if a person does not do A, then B will happen. In either case, B is a very, very bad thing. These types of arguments become fallacies, as Gula points out, when they fail to show any actual causal relationship between A and B.[19] Arguing, for example, that your university should not build a new gymnasium because then tuition will go up and students will have to drop out is an argument from fear. After all, new gymnasiums are usually donor funded. Other examples include arguing that if you do not take certain actions against climate change, violent storms will destroy your hometown. Or if we do not increase border security, violent crime will increase in the United States. These things may be true, but the arguer would need to produce evidence demonstrating causal connections.

Another variation on the argument from fear is the *argumentum ad baculum*, or *argument from the rod (baculum)*, or coercion. Ancient Romans gathered rods together into tied bundles called fasces, which symbolized power. Indeed, the modern ideology of fascism derives its name from Roman fasces and the order they supposedly represented. In this informal fallacy, the thuggish arguer again refuses to engage with the content of the argument and instead demands silence or submission by threatening to use force. We see the argument from coercion deployed in practice when speakers are driven from their platforms under threat of violence. This happened, for example, to controversial libertarian social scientist Charles Murray at Middlebury College in Vermont on March 2, 2017. Protests forced progressive political science professor Allison Stanger to interview Murray off-stage via closed circuit broadcast. However, protests became increasingly violent following the interview and Stanger suffered a neck injury and concussion. The incident inspired the conservative professor Robert P. George and the progressive professor Cornel West to pen a joint statement on "Truth Seeking, Democracy, and Freedom of Thought and Expression." In it, George, West, and later signatories called on readers to respectfully engage with the arguments of opponents, rather than

questioning the motives and thus stigmatizing those who dissent from prevailing opinions [circumstantial *ad hominem*]; or by disrupting their presentations; or by demanding that they be excluded from campus or, if they have already been invited, disinvited [*argumentum ad baculum*]. Sometimes students and faculty members turn their backs on speakers whose opinions they don't like or simply walk out and refuse to listen to those whose convictions offend their values. Of course, the right to peacefully protest, including on campuses, is sacrosanct. But before exercising that right, each of us should ask: Might it not be better to listen respectfully and try to learn from a speaker with whom I disagree? Might it better serve the cause of truth-seeking to engage the speaker in frank civil discussion?[20]

George, West, and the other signatories are correct. Without listening (or reading) respectfully and learning from our dialog partner, how can we discern truth from error?

Aesthetic Fallacy: But It's So Pretty!

Sometimes good – or bad – looks can be distracting. Anyone who has ever spent any time on a beach is aware of this fact. Hence the adage "don't judge a book by its cover." This has become truer than ever in our highly visual age. We're not just reading books with black-and-white text; we're also spending more time than ever reading text embedded in beautifully designed websites. Sometimes the aesthetic – or beauty – appeal of a source can make readers assume its content is more accurate than it really is. It can also draw attention away from shoddy arguments. The same is true of websites and texts that "look" academic, perhaps because of a slick layout or the heavy use of citations. Interestingly, one study determined that when asked to evaluate the reliability of web sources, students were primarily concerned with how academic a site looked as opposed to other factors. According to Professor Donald Leu, "'We were quite surprised that none of the students did anything to evaluate the site. That is, they didn't Google it, they didn't try and locate who the author was, try and determine who had created this' (Cherry, 2011). It was as if the students assumed that since the site had lots of text-based information presented in an academic-looking format, 'it must be reliable and I can use it in my homework.'"[21] Alas, for these students, academic appearance does not always entail academic content. For example, the website of a center or institute that believes President John F. Kennedy was assassinated because of a government conspiracy may appear credible because of its professional design, but you should also ask if it contains reliable content. In this case, you'd want to look for something like citations to peer-reviewed studies conducted by experts with credentials in relevant subfields, like American political history.

The *aesthetic fallacy* doesn't just apply to websites, either; it also applies to physical books and journals. One way that shoddy or dishonest scholars, like Holocaust deniers, attempt to convince others is by cramming their books full of footnotes and the technical apparatus of academic writing.[22] As a result, the arguments *appear* to be well researched and based on plenty of hard evidence. But looks can be deceiving. The reader needs to investigate to see what sources are actually cited and how they are used. The key here is to not be distracted by a website's flashy design or a book's copious footnotes or glossy illustrations. All that really matters is the argument.

The Bandwagon: Don't Jump on It

Appeals to authority can also be tied up with what Gula calls "snob appeal."[23] We want to be associated with the smartest, wealthiest, and most famous people, so we use their names to lend authority to our arguments. Basically, we're trying to make our arguments look better by hanging out with the elites, the cool kids. The populist version of this tendency is the *bandwagon fallacy*. This fallacy assumes that because lots of people agree about something, they must be right. For example, someone living in the 1500s could argue that most natural philosophers and common people agree that the earth occupies the central position in the solar system. Therefore, it must be true that we live in a geocentric universe. The assumption here is that if everyone is doing or buying something, it must be the right thing to do. So jump on the bandwagon – it's a safe, happy ride full of straw and pumpkins! The bandwagon appeal is related to the *argumentum ad populum*, or *appeal to the people*. Here the arguer diverts attention away from the argument and evidence and toward the opinion of the crowd. However, do not assume that just because most people, even your friends, agree about a certain interpretation, they are necessarily correct.[24]

Appeal to Tradition

Yet another version of the appeal to the people's authority is the *appeal to tradition or antiquity (argumentum ad antiquitatem)*. This extends the appeal to authority back in time and is more likely to appeal to the emotions of conservatives. When appealing to tradition, a person argues that she is correct because such and such has always been done a certain way. In other words, the majority of people, when considered across all of time, agree with the arguer. Roman Catholic apologist G.K. Chesterton famously defined "tradition" in this way as "the democracy of the dead": "Tradition means giving a vote to most obscure of all classes, our ancestors. It is the democracy of the dead. Tradition refuses to submit to the small and arrogant oligarchy of those who merely happen to be walking about."[25] So, one might argue that we should not change the legal definition of marriage because marriage has traditionally been defined only as being between one man and one woman, regardless of what the majority might think now. Or, one might argue that we need to return to naturopathic medicine because it has a more ancient pedigree than modern medicine. Now, there may very well be good reasons to uphold the traditional definition of marriage or practice naturalistic medicine. But the fact that it has always been done that way or that it was done that way for a long time is not a good reason in and of itself. The present differs from the past, and as a result, the authority of tradition may be at least partially irrelevant. To determine whether that is the case or not, an arguer would need to bring in additional evidence.

Sunk-Cost Fallacy

Another diversionary fallacy is the infamous *sunk-cost fallacy*. In this fallacy, you assume that because you have already invested so much of something into a cause, you cannot reverse course since to do so could mean all your previous investments had been in vain. This emotional response distracts you from rationally considering a situation. You might encounter the sunk-cost fallacy if you begin a particularly difficult class in astronomy and invest a great deal of time and effort studying. Despite your best efforts, however, it becomes clear that you are not going to pass the class. Your advisor recommends that you drop the course and pick up another that is more suited to your interests. However, given that you'd already invested so much in the astronomy course, wouldn't you feel hesitant to drop it? While this feeling is understandable, it is also based on the sunk-cost fallacy. Having put a lot into something in no way necessitates continuing to do so, especially if doing so is against your interests. We see this fallacy quite frequently in debates about public policy. Someone may argue that we can't end subsidies to green energy sources because we've already invested too much money in building up the industry. Or another person could say that we can't pull American soldiers out of the war in Afghanistan because we have already lost over two thousand soldiers. Therefore, their sacrifice would be in vain if we left the conflict before achieving total military victory. In both cases, the erroneous assumption is that sunk costs must determine future actions.

Linguistic Diversions

Etymological Fallacies: It Doesn't Mean What You Think

The *etymological fallacy* assumes that a word (like "nice") meant the same thing in the past that it does today. Etymology – not to be confused with the study of insects, or entomology – is the study of the origin of words and their development. Not surprisingly then, in this fallacy, the arguer uses the origin or development of a word to discredit an opponent even though the word's origin is completely irrelevant to the argument. This is a form of equivocation. Again, this strategy can distract the opponent, who then finds himself caught in a tangle over word origins instead of evidence. For example, the word "nice" originates in the Latin *nescius*, or ignorant. In response to the comment, "Dr. Kilcrease is a nice woman," someone could reply, "that means you're really saying she's ignorant." Of course, the speaker did not intend for the word nice to mean ignorant, but now he finds himself on the defensive. Another type of etymological fallacy tries to create irrelevant associations between words on the basis of etymology or translation. For example, religious fundamentalists may note that many scholars translate the biblical Greek word *pharmakeia*, which referred to magic produced using drugs, as "sorcery."[26] This means that pharmacology and sorcery are directly related! Therefore, modern pharmaceutical medicine is witchcraft and religious believers should avoid it. In reality, however, the etymological fallacy just distracts from the lack of evidence supporting a real connection between sorcery and modern medicine.

The Word Concept Fallacy

Sometimes the etymological fallacy is related to the problem of anachronism and also to what historian Carl Trueman calls the *word concept fallacy*.[27] The word concept fallacy assumes that a word in a historical text (like "conservative") meant the same thing in the past that it means today.[28] Or, more broadly, this fallacy assumes or gives the false impression that a word has the same definition in any context. When writing, you need to consider exactly which definition of a word you intend to use. Then, be sure to make this clear to the reader to avoid equivocation. I accidentally fell into this error myself in my first book when I failed to adequately explain exactly which definition of the word "Erastian" I was using at different times. Obviously I did not intend to confuse readers, but I apparently did.

Unfortunately, some unscrupulous individuals intentionally confuse the definition of certain words in order to win an argument. Therefore, the burden ultimately falls on the reader or listener to discern how a given word is being used. For example, if an American today starts claiming to be advancing liberal policy, but actually believes in small government and laissez-faire economics, she may be unintentionally or intentionally tripping into the word concept fallacy. In the nineteenth century, liberals advocated for small government and laissez-faire economics. In Europe, politicians holding these positions are often still known as liberals. But in the United States, politicians and the general public now usually apply the moniker "liberal" to politicians supporting big government and more intervention in the economy. In fact, the ideology referred to as liberalism in nineteenth-century Europe is now in many ways closer to contemporary American conservatism. Definitions change over time and vary based on context.

Pseudo-Profundity

In the *fallacy of pseudo-profundity*, something looks profound because it is expressed in big words, but it's really gibberish. Or perhaps it's not purely meaningless, but the meaning is obscured either intentionally or unintentionally by jargon. Academics may fall into this informal fallacy more than other professionals do. Victoria Clayton recently wrote an article for the *Atlantic* entitled "The Needless Complexity of Academic Writing," in which she discusses the problem of opaque scholarly writing and the movement to increase its clarity. Clayton highlights the following excerpt from Barbara Vinken's *Flaubert Postsecular: Modernity Crossed Out* (Oxford University Press, 2015) as an example of writing that has become dense to the point of becoming unintelligible gobbledygook:

> The work of the text is to literalize the signifiers of the first encounter, dismantling the ideal as an idol. In this literalization, the idolatrous deception of the first moment becomes readable. The ideal will reveal

itself to be an idol. Step by step, the ideal is pursued by a devouring doppelganger, tearing apart all transcendence. This de-idealization follows the path of reification, or, to invoke Augustine, the path of carnalization of the spiritual. Rhetorically, this is effected through literalization. *A Sentimental Education* does little more than elaborate the progressive literalization of the Annunciation.[29]

Now, it needs to be said that the content of Vinken's work has been well received by literary scholars and so, underneath the torturous prose, it does contain intelligible and insightful ideas. However, this is not always the case.

Many have criticized academic writing, especially postmodern or poststructuralist writing, as being fundamentally nothing but pseudo-profound gibberish. It may look deep because of all the big words, but really it means nothing. Infamously, in 1996 scientist Alan Sokal sought to reveal the pseudo-profound nature of postmodern academic writing by submitting an article entitled "Transgressing the Boundaries: Towards a Transformative Hermeneutics of Quantum Gravity" to the cultural studies journal *Social Text*. *Social Text* published the paper despite the fact that Sokal had deliberately written nonsense under the cover of fashionably turgid postmodern academic prose. The Sokal Affair, as it came to be known, revealed that even academics, like the editor of *Social Text*, can be duped by pseudo-profundity. Just because something uses seemingly "profound" language doesn't mean the author is smarter than you. The big words and convoluted sentence constructions could be an intentional or unintentional attempt to make a simple argument look more sophisticated or to cover up a nonsensical argument without real evidence.

Fallacies of Ambiguity: Vagueness

Pseudo-profundity can give rise to ambiguity, which is itself a very common category of informal fallacies. When an arguer uses vague or imprecise language, rebuttal or even understanding becomes difficult. For example, one might argue, "We need to do something about the US debt, because it's huge!" But what does "do something" mean? And how much is "huge"? How can you even respond to such a proposal? "Something" is too vague to either agree or disagree with. "Huge" is a relative term. What is an unmanageably large amount to you might still be acceptable to someone else. Your brother might see no problem with racking up $25,000 in credit card debt, whereas such a fiscal situation would bring you to the brink of despair. In this case, rather than "do something," the arguer needs to propose a specific line of action. He also needs to replace "huge" with a quantifiable figure. In my experience, vague or imprecise language often mars student papers and thesis statements. Students may argue that the American Revolution was successful or that a certain thing or book was influential. But what do these words and concepts actually mean? This problem is hardly limited to student papers, though. We need to keep in mind that strong arguments always clearly define their terms, and ill-defined terms could signal fallacious reasoning.

Of course, not just words themselves can be ambiguous. The position of words in sentences or grammatical constructions can be ambiguous as well. Here's a fun word: amphiboly. An amphiboly occurs when the placement of a word in a sentence leads to ambiguous meaning. The classic example of an amphiboly is "Last night I caught a thief in my pajamas." So, were you wearing your pajamas when you caught the thief, or did the thief steal and then put on your pajamas before being caught? To clarify, the writer might revise the sentence to "Last night in my pajamas I caught a thief." Be careful not to use an amphiboly when making arguments as well. Don't write "I oppose Environmental Protection Agency deregulations which hurt the environment." Does this mean that you oppose *all* EPA deregulations since they always hurt the environment? Or do you *only* oppose those deregulations that hurt the environment?[30] Be sure to punctuate properly and clarify your meaning.

Another more specific type of argument that tends to slip into ambiguity is the appeal to nature.[31] We see this constantly in advertising and in the health-care industry today. Marketers argue that their product is the best because it is the most natural. Why buy organic foods? They are natural. Why seek out non-GMO foods? Again, they are the most natural. But what does "natural" mean? Given that humans have been genetically manipulating foodstuffs since the domestication of crops, where do we draw the line between natural non-GMO foods and artificial GMO foods? We also see this in the craze for essential oils. Have a headache? Feel stressed? Don't reach for an artificial pill. Instead, release a drop of all-natural lavender essential oil. Purveyors of said oils argue that their wares are better than popping an aspirin or a valium because oils are natural. Now, this may all be true. Perhaps these products are better than the alternatives. However, just because something is natural does not make it necessarily better than a rival product. Having a grizzly bear eat you is also a perfectly natural occurrence. Nevertheless, I suspect it's one we'd all want to avoid! Natural is not synonymous with good.

Quote Mining

Another fallacy of ambiguity is *selective quoting*, or *quote mining*. In this case, an arguer uses a quotation as evidence without providing the appropriate context. This usage renders the meaning of the evidence ambiguous. As a professor, I see this fallacy frequently in student papers. As we have seen, this informal fallacy is often paired with appeals to irrelevant authority. An arguer will search for a quotation by a famous individual and use that to bolster his or her position without concern for the quotation's original meaning or context. For example, a student may argue against further gun control legislation by quoting Thomas Jefferson: "the tree of liberty must be refreshed from time to time with the blood of patriots & tyrants. It is it's [*sic*] natural manure."[32] This student then argues that, on the authority of Founding Father Thomas Jefferson, the tree of liberty needs to be periodically refreshed. Therefore, individuals need quick and easy access to arms in order to defend themselves. Thus, further gun control legislation is unwise. Supposing this quotation is authentic – and it is – does it fully support the arguer's position? The context of Jefferson's remark was discussion of a draft of the new American constitution and an early outburst of discontent that would eventually become Shays' Rebellion against Massachusetts. Rather than regard the rebels as righteous defenders of liberty, however, Jefferson argued that they promoted very distasteful anarchy, despite the fact that they acted out of ignorance as opposed to wickedness.[33] Jefferson was never a supporter of anarchic individualism. The student would need to explain Jefferson's quotation in a more nuanced manner, while also addressing the possible informal fallacies of appealing to past authority and anachronism, since we can't apply our concerns to Jefferson's times and then use Jefferson's authority to support one side or another in our own political battles.

Equivocation

Another type of fallacy of ambiguity is *equivocation*. Broadly, equivocation refers to using language in an ambiguous way, often to avoid telling the truth. So you equivocate when you use one word or phrase in different ways in an argument or discussion.[34] For example, you might tell your parents that you are "going out with a friend" on a Saturday night. Your parents assume you are going out to study with a platonic friend, but in reality, you are going out with your significant other. You might reason that you didn't lie per se. Your parents just *assumed* that the friendship in question was a platonic one. If an antifeminist politician speaks to a group on his way to the broadly feminist Women's March and says he supports a vague thing called "social justice," you may wonder if the politician is equivocating to gain a favorable reception. Listeners may assume the speaker is promoting one definition of social justice that involves support for benefits like federally mandated maternity leave. On the other hand, the speaker may be using the term social justice in a different way that places more emphasis on the freedom of employers to determine the extent of maternity leave. In this example, both the speaker and the audience leave happy and believing that they agree on the topic of social justice when in fact substantial disagreements remain. Coming to true understanding, then, requires clear definitions without equivocation.

Category Confusion: Apples Aren't Oranges

A final fallacy of ambiguity is the so-called *apples and oranges fallacy*, or *category confusion*. In this fallacy, "two things are compared or contrasted that are actually incomparable."[35] This fallacy creates ambiguity over the equivalency of the two incomparable things compared. This is the problem of comparing apples and oranges. You may try, but you simply can't do it. Which is better? A new smartphone or a new coffeemaker? Who knows? How can you compare the two? Personally, I'll take both! Someone may argue that you need to also support reduced sentences for possession of illegal firearms if you support reduced sentences for possession of marijuana. This argument does not work, however, since possession of illegal firearms and possession of illegal marijuana are not readily comparable without further explanation. The two are apples and oranges.

You should also beware a reverse version of the apples and oranges fallacy. Sometimes someone will claim that they have two incomparable things when really they are the same. For example, in the 1980s the United States Congress passed minimum sentencing laws for drug-related offenses. This legislation made the minimum mandatory sentence for the possession of crack cocaine significantly higher than that of any other drug, including powder cocaine. However, cocaine is cocaine regardless of the form in which it is consumed.[36] In this case, legislators were influenced by extraneous factors and failed to see that crack cocaine and powder cocaine weren't apples and oranges; they were apples and apples and therefore the same sentencing should apply. Congress finally began to address this disparity in the Fair Sentencing Act of 2010 under President Barack Obama's administration.

As we wrap up our deep dive into the world of fallacies, both formal and informal, it's worth considering one final informal fallacy: the *fallacy fallacy!*[37] Now that you know so much about fallacies and how to spot them, you are even more vulnerable to the meta fallacy fallacy, which supposes that because an argument is fallacious the conclusion it intends to support is false. Fallacies tell us nothing about whether the conclusion is actually true or false. They only tell us that the conclusion does not necessarily follow from this (fallacious) reasoning. Fallacies are only the means through which we can fall into errors, and their existence does not necessarily show a position is false. In fact, to assume that nothing truthful could come out of a source with a fallacy would be to commit a version of the genetic fallacy. An argument could ultimately be correct despite containing a fallacy. So, on the one hand, be diligent in finding and defusing fallacies. But on the other hand, do not assume that you can ignore an argument or source just because you uncover a single logical flaw. The fact that someone employs a fallacy in defense of the need for critical thinking skills in college education curriculum does not mean critical thinking skills are not needed in a college education curriculum!

Logical Fallacy Exercises

Now that you've learned about them, can you pick out the logical fallacies in the sentences below? Which logical fallacy or fallacies do you think each sentence contains? Why did you answer the way you did? You can pick the same fallacy more than once.

Fallacy Term Bank: abusive ad hominem, appeal to emotion, appeal to irrelevant authority, appeal to tradition, argument from fear, bandwagon fallacy, circumstantial ad hominem, equivocation, etymological fallacy, guilt by association, pseudo-profundity, sacred cow, scapegoat fallacy, special pleading, straw man fallacy, *tu quoque* fallacy, "two wrongs make a right" fallacy, vague appeal to authority, vagueness, word concept fallacy

1) Joe: "Dante's *Divine Comedy* is a significant piece of Italian literature and should be taught to all first-year college students."
   Ken: "The *Divine Comedy* can't be important to teach to students because it's not even funny."
2) Donald Trump may have committed sexual assault. However, Hillary Clinton also may have helped cover up Bill Clinton's sexual indiscretions, so that means we can't condemn Trump.
3) I should get an extension on my research paper despite the fact that no one else did.
4) Joe to Kevin: "You're only supporting the Keystone Pipeline because of your ties to the oil industry."
5) Just think of how the wealthiest 1 per cent of Americans live in fancy houses with golden toilets and grind the poor under the soles of their designer shoes! The oppressed poor cry out for justice! Therefore, we need higher income taxes.
6) If same-sex marriage continues to be legal in the United States, then the courts are sure to legalize pedophilia.
7) Bob: "I think we should place more restrictions on the purchase of semiautomatic rifles."
   Joe: "The right to bear arms ensures our political liberty. How dare you attack our freedoms, Bob!"

8) Hillary Clinton may have improperly handled classified documents. However, Donald Trump probably colluded with the Russians to influence the 2016 presidential election. Therefore, we can't condemn Clinton.

9) Contemporary American conservatives cannot possibly oppose free trade because under President Ronald Reagan, conservatives supported free trade.

10) But how can Pastor Jones condemn me for the sin of covetousness? He's a sinner too.

11) If the president nominates a conservative justice for the Supreme Court, women will lose their reproductive rights.

12) We should not vote for any immoral presidential candidates. Although I admit that my candidate violates my personal moral code, I'm going to vote for her anyway.

13) Inequality is a big problem.

14) After arising from sweet slumber and sauntering to the hallowed halls of pedagogy for a period of instruction, I plan to enjoy a brief repast with my comrades.

15) Joe: "I think we need to end affirmation action and return to color-blind approaches to college admissions and hiring practices."
    Bob: "Affirmative action is necessary to rectify structural racial inequalities. Are you opposed to equality, Joe?"

16) Bethany Kilcrease, professor of history, argues that the 100th Street Bridge is structurally sound and, therefore, it is perfectly safe to drive over it with very heavy trucks.

17) Most people think chocolate is tasty! Therefore, it must be objectively delicious because all those people can't be wrong.

18) Scholars claim that *Lord of the Rings* is the greatest fantasy trilogy of all time.

19) Sue: "We can't change the rules to speed up Major League Baseball games!"
    Kate: "Why not?"
    Sue: "Because baseball has always been a slow game."

20) Roman Catholics want to control women's sexuality, so they oppose abortion and artificial birth control.

21) Philosophers say knowledge is power, and philosophers have a lot of knowledge. Why don't they win all the powerlifting competitions then?

22) There is a lot of crime. Immigrants are to blame for this. Therefore, if we get rid of immigrants we can solve the problem of crime.

23) Intolerance is a problem in America. Evangelical Christians are to blame. Therefore, if we limit freedom of religion for Evangelicals in the public square, we'll have much less intolerance.

24) President George W. Bush only launched the 2003 war in Iraq to obtain access to Iraqi oil.

25) From a student evaluation: "My biology professor wears ugly sweaters. Therefore, she grades unfairly."

26) All your family and friends belong to a fundamentalist religious sect. Therefore, you must also be a fundamentalist and reject evolutionary biology.

27) Dentists claim that "Sparkly White" toothpaste will get your teeth whiter than any other brand.

28) The advertisement for these pain pills says they will make arthritic joints vanish. Therefore, you shouldn't take them, because you don't want your knees to vanish.

Answers

1) This is an etymological fallacy. The epic's title identifies it as a "comedy" because it ends happily. But Ken is using the modern definition of comedy as something funny. The development of the word "comedy" from meaning a story that ends happily to something funny merely distracts from the argument that the *Divine Comedy* should be taught in college.

2) This is the "two wrongs make a right" fallacy. The fact that Clinton may have done a bad thing does not lessen the gravity of the wrong possibly committed by Trump.

3) This is special pleading if the student does not give any reasons why he or she should receive an extension.

4) This is a circumstantial ad hominem fallacy. Joe is trying to discredit Kevin by attacking his possible motives, not his arguments.

5) This is an appeal to emotion. The image of wealthy and powerful individuals oppressing the poor and needy (probably?) evokes strong emotions.

6) This argument from fear uses fear of pedophilia to make an argument against LGBTQ+ marriage. Note that this argument can also take the form of the slippery slope on occasion.

7) Here Joe is making a sacred cow out of liberty or freedom. This distracts from the real argument about semiautomatic rifles.

8) This is the "two wrongs make a right" fallacy. The fact that Trump may have done a bad thing does not lessen the gravity of the wrong possibly committed by Clinton.

9) This is an example of the word concept fallacy, which is a type of etymological fallacy. The definition of "conservativism" in an American context has changed over time. Reagan conservatives generally supported free trade, whereas, increasingly, many Trump conservatives support economic nationalism and protectionism.

10) This is the *tu quoque* fallacy because calling Pastor Jones a hypocrite does not logically negate his argument.

11) This argument from fear uses fear of losing reproductive rights to make an argument against conservative justices.

12) This is special pleading unless there is a compelling reason why the individual would vote for this particular immoral person but not any others.

13) This argument is too vague. What kind of inequality? Economic? Social? Political? What exactly does "big" mean here?

14) This is pseudo-profundity because the speaker either intentionally or unintentionally obscures meaning with profound words. The author could more simply have said, "After waking up and walking to the academic building for class, I plan on going to lunch with friends."

15) Here Bob is making a sacred cow out of equality. This distracts from the real argument about affirmative action.

16) This is an appeal to irrelevant authority. Since I am a history professor and not an engineer in the relevant subfield, there is no reason to think I know better than anyone else whether or not the bridge is structurally sound.

17) This is a bandwagon fallacy. Just because a lot of people agree about something doesn't mean they are right.

18) This is a vague appeal to authority. Which scholars? How many? The arguer should be more specific. Moreover, this could also be an appeal to irrelevant authority. Perhaps the scholars in question are chemists as opposed to literary scholars.

19) This is an appeal to tradition. Sue is arguing that the age or tradition associated with something puts it beyond question.

20) Aside from generalizing about Roman Catholics, this argument commits the straw man fallacy because saying that Roman Catholics oppose abortion access and some forms of birth control because they oppose women's sexuality misrepresents their actual arguments.

21) This is the fallacy of equivocation. The word "power" in the phrase "knowledge is power" does not refer to the physical strength required to excel in the sport of powerlifting.

22) This is a scapegoat fallacy. Here immigrants are being used as a scapegoat for high crime rates.

23) This is a scapegoat fallacy. Here Evangelical Christians are being used as a scapegoat for intolerance.

24) This is a circumstantial ad hominem fallacy because it attacks President Bush's possible motives, not his actual arguments.

25) In addition to being a non sequitur, this is an abusive ad hominem argument. The student is attacking the biology professor herself, not any evidence or arguments relative to grading.

26) This is the fallacy of guilt by association. The argument that a person must be guilty of rejecting evolutionary biology by virtue of her family's religious connections is a type of guilt by association.

27) This is a vague appeal to authority. Which dentists? How many? The arguer should be more specific.

28) This is the fallacy of equivocation. The word "vanish" is being used in an ambiguous way. The advertisement means the pills will ease the symptoms of arthritis, not make physical joints literally disappear into some type of wormhole.

Find the Fallacies Essay Scavenger Hunt

Here is a sample of student writing. Try to pick out as many logical fallacies from the previous three chapters as you can and determine why they are logical fallacies.

The eighteenth century was a tumultuous time across the Atlantic world. Two of the most significant events were the American and French Revolutions. Both of these revolutions involved a lot of fighting and bloodshed. In the end, however, new forms of government emerged in both America and France. The American Revolution (1775–83) obviously caused the French Revolution (1789–1815), since the French Revolution only occurred after the American Revolution. However, since older things are always better, the French Revolution was worse than the American Revolution. As Dr. Jimmy Smith, MD, says, "I think the French Revolution was no good!" This is because the leaders of the French Revolution, like Robespierre, were terrible people and motivated by their anger and hatred of humanity. Robespierre led the Committee of Public Safety to initiate the Terror, which killed thousands of innocent French citizens on trumped-up charges. Since the Terror of 1794–95 was bad, the entire French Revolution was a bad event. In fact, the French should have never attempted to reform their political system in the first place because creating a perfect governing system is impossible.

Find the Fallacies Essay Scavenger Hunt – Answers

1) "The American Revolution (1775–83) obviously caused the French Revolution (1789–1815), since the French Revolution only occurred after the American Revolution."

This is the *post hoc, ergo propter hoc* (after this, therefore because of this) fallacy. Just because the French Revolution occurred after the American Revolution, the American Revolution did not necessarily cause the French Revolution. There could be a temporal correlation between the two events without there being a causal relationship.

2) "However, since older things are always better, the French Revolution was worse than the American Revolution."

This is the appeal to tradition fallacy. Things are not necessarily good or better or correct just by virtue of being traditional or older. The term "better" is also vague. Better how? The author should define what he or she means by "better."

3) "As Dr. Jimmy Smith, MD, says, 'I think the French Revolution was no good.'"

This is an appeal to irrelevant authority. Having a medical degree (like an MD) does not make one an authority on the French Revolution. "No good" is also vague.

4) "This is because the leaders of the French Revolution, like Robespierre, were terrible people and motivated by their anger and hatred of humanity."

This is an oversimplification. The characters of the leaders of the French Revolution did not solely determine its outcome. This sentence also contains an abusive ad hominem fallacy. It attacks the character of the leaders of the French Revolution rather than the arguments that may have fueled their decisions. Finally, the ad hominem argument is also circumstantial because it argues the French Revolution was "no good" based on the motivations of Robespierre and others rather than their arguments or actions.

5) "Since the Terror of 1794–95 was bad, the entire French Revolution was a bad event."

This is a fallacy of composition. The argument takes one bad part of the whole French Revolution and then says the whole thing was "bad" based on that one part. Note that "bad" is also a vague term.

6) "In fact, the French should have never attempted to reform their political system in the first place because creating a perfect governing system is impossible."

This is the nirvana fallacy. The arguer is saying that since the French couldn't possibly implement a *perfect* new government, they should never have attempted to reform their old one. But the inability to do something perfectly does not mean it should never be attempted.

PART III

BRINGING IT TOGETHER

CHAPTER 9

WRITING ABOUT ANYTHING

Regardless of your major, one of the things you'll get to do in college is write papers. And this is good news, because if there is ever a time for undergraduate students to develop into stronger writers, this is it. If there's one thing professors should agree on, it's this: writing forces students to think about their own positions more clearly, examine evidence more critically, and learn to both understand and empathize with the positions of others. As Fareed Zakaria notes in his book *In Defense of a Liberal Education*, "the central virtue of a liberal education is that it teaches you how to write, and writing makes you think."[1] Yes, employers obviously value skills like strong writing, as I pointed out in chapter 2. But, again, promoting the common good via participation in democratic society also requires these skills.

You are undoubtedly familiar with the partisan rancor permeating contemporary American society. In a world saturated with social networking you may experience these political and cultural divisions, and the arguments that come with them, largely through the internet. Yes, Uncle Joe and Cousin Sally still argue over the cranberry sauce every Thanksgiving about merits and demerits of single-payer health care or LGBTQ+ rights, but given the amount of time we spend online today, you probably encounter heated partisan rhetoric more often on Instagram, Twitter, Facebook, or another platform. We've already examined how you can evaluate the types of sources and arguments you may find either in print or on the internet. Now is the time to wade into the debate yourself, by exploring how to craft and write out your own thoughts or findings. Learning to carefully construct an argument based on evidence and to respectfully join a larger discussion on a given topic, even a controversial one, strengthens your skill set and benefits society.

Writing

After that lofty preamble, let's get down to the actual task of writing papers in college. What follows are some general guidelines and hazards to avoid, which apply to many common nonfiction writing assignments involving research. While I hope this short survey of writing will prove helpful, you should always be sure to conform your writing to the guidelines your professor will give you for any specific assignment. I'm a history professor, so much of what I say will come from that perspective. It will therefore apply most directly to the types of writing assignments you might receive in a humanities or social science course. Of course, you won't only take history classes and your assignments will take many different forms. History papers, for example, will be different than biology lab reports. Regardless, though, commonalities exist among all the different types of writing you'll be doing. One of the first hazards you'll need to avoid is writing without an intended audience in mind. If your audience is unclear, you should ask your professor for clarification. I usually tell my students that the primary audience of their papers is educated individuals who are nevertheless not experts, like their classmates. Therefore, when in doubt, my students need to *explain* things in their papers, not just assume I will know what they're talking about because I have a degree in history. Of course, other professors, like your biology professor, may assume a different audience for your writing. Regardless of the assignment, be sure to know for whom you're writing before you begin.

Another similarity among many college writing assignments is the need to select a subject and then ask a question about it. Every piece of writing results from someone asking some type of question about a subject, even if the subject and question are only implicit. Why do birds migrate south? Why do the Kurdish people want their own nation-state? What ingredients do I need to buy to make dinner tonight? And so on. Be sure you have a question to focus your research and writing. Papers without a clear question quickly meander away from their topics. You might have to come up with the question your paper will answer on your own, or your professor might give you a question to answer. In either case, the goal of your paper is to answer that question. The first paragraph or paragraphs should introduce both your subject and your question or goal.

The Introduction

Common Writing Hazards to Avoid

- Being unaware of the audience or context
- Lacking a question about a topic
- Lacking a thesis or answer to that question
- Saving the thesis for the conclusion (unless this is appropriate to the assignment)
- Lacking a blueprint or introductory road map
- Failure to integrate and explain sources
- Failure to include a conclusion
- Not enough analysis
- Attempting to write in a voice other than your own

Your answer to this question is the paper's thesis, or central argument. Therefore, the thing most academic writing assignments have in common is the need for some kind of explicit answer to a question. In fact, as we have seen in chapter 5, another way of thinking about the arguments made in papers and presentations is as answers to a question. Because providing an answer to your question is so important, failure to include a thesis is perhaps the greatest pitfall to avoid. This holds true across disciplines. While humanities and social science papers obviously need to include arguments, even lab manuscripts must include findings. Of course, some types of writing, like journalistic reporting, do try to avoid making an argument or interpreting the facts for the audience. Nevertheless, even journalists are answering the "who, what, where, why" questions. Additionally, journalists also start their writing with introductory sections that explain the main points of the story in shorthand for the reader before then getting into the nitty-gritty factual details.

So every paper needs to include a thesis, findings, or at minimum some kind of main points. But where should you place this element in your paper? Generally, a thesis or the main point should go toward the end of your initial introduction paragraph. It's usually a bit much for the reader to take in if you immediately begin your paper with the thesis. So, again, give your reader a few sentences of background and the necessary context about your subject before writing your thesis. My students tend to write their theses as the last sentences of the introduction paragraph, but that doesn't necessarily have to be the case.

This brings us to the issue of so-called spoilers in argumentative papers. In the past, when I've told students that they need to put their conclusions in the first paragraph, some have found this disconcerting. Putting your argument, or what you conclude, in the first paragraph seems like a spoiler. After all, why read to the end of a paper if you already know the conclusion after reading only one paragraph? Frankly, this is a very astute observation when it comes to many types of writing. As a great lover of old British detective stories, I would be very disappointed if Agatha Christie revealed who had committed the murder on the first page. However, historical writing is different than a detective novel. Scholars like your professors actually *want* to know your entire argument and how you will make it after having read only one page. We want spoilers! The introduction of an academic paper functions like an executive summary of a lengthy report. It gives you the argument right up front. The exciting thing for professors is not reading the whole paper to find out what the argument will be. The exciting thing – since the argument has *already* appeared in the introduction – is finding out if the writer has effectively marshaled enough evidence to make the reader agree with the argument. The goal is to win the reader over to your side.

Every paper, then, needs an introduction paragraph that tells the reader about your topic and usually introduces your question and answer. As we've seen, this paragraph usually starts with some general context or background relating to the subject about which you are asking a question. It then ends with your argument, findings, or main point(s). This is the most important part of the whole paper, so be sure not to forget it. This sentence (or sentences) needs to be clear, direct, specific, and – ideally it if is a true thesis – original. Immediately prior to this sentence, immediately following it, or as a part of it, you should tell the reader what categories of evidence or points you will bring up to support your argument. This will inform your readers *where* your paper will go and *how* you arrived at the answer you did. I sometimes call this the blueprint sentence or sentences, because it maps the construction of your entire paper so the reader knows what to expect. Carol Berkin, in *The History Handbook*, puts it this way: "You must ... detail the most important points you plan to make in the paper, so that you give the reader a guideline to follow."[2]

Let's take a look at an example from my field of British history. Suppose the question you are answering is "What caused the English Civil War?" Your argumentative answer (thesis) might be: "The English Civil War was directly caused by financial difficulties and only indirectly caused by political and cultural disagreements between the monarchy and Parliament." Note that we could also say – using the language about causation we learned in the previous chapter – that finances were a direct agent cause, whereas political/cultural conflict was a necessary cause. Leaving that alone, however, the reader now knows you will argue that financial problems, and not political/cultural conflict, are what most directly caused the Civil War. But your reader still doesn't know *how* you will support that argument. Therefore, tell the reader what specific points you are going to make to prove your thesis. For example: "Political and cultural tension between Stuart royalists and Parliamentarians formed part of the background of the Civil War. However, debt inherited from the Tudor Dynasty and Charles I's attempt to raise money without Parliament for eleven years caused even more conflict. Most immediately, Charles's attempt to raise money through Parliament to fight Scotland in 1639 and 1640 triggered the Civil War in England."

So, on the basis of these thesis and blueprint sentences, I know that you'll be arguing that the English Civil War was really most immediately caused by financial difficulties, not political or cultural conflict. I also know that to make your argument, you're first going to discuss the fact that political and cultural conflict obviously did play at least a background role in the Civil War. But then you'll explain that financial problems, specifically those caused by inherited debt and Charles's attempts to raise money, were more important in the buildup to the war. Finally, you'll explain that it was Charles's need for money to fight the Scottish Bishops' War that most directly triggered the open conflict between King and Parliament.

A strong thesis and introduction paragraph tells the reader what you will argue and how you will make that argument. But, again, you can't expect your reader to just take your word for it that you've given the correct answer to the question at hand. For example, you can't assume that your reader will automatically believe you that financial trouble was the primary cause of the English Civil War. Maybe your reader thinks the anti-Catholicism of John Pym and other Puritans most directly caused the conflict. Given that actual fighting didn't break out until 1642, someone may argue that financial difficulties arising in 1640 are too distant to be a direct agent cause and, instead, conflict between King and Parliament over raising an army to fight rebels in Ireland in late 1641 was the immediate cause. In any case, because your audience can plausibly disagree with your interpretation, you need to convince your reader that it was really all about money. As a result, after the introduction paragraph, the point of the body of the paper is to stack up enough evidence or data to prove your case and thereby convince your reader that your argument is correct. It's like being a lawyer arguing a case.

Evidence and Argumentation

Just like lawyers, or detectives, historians and other scholars – yourself included – need to find evidence to prove their cases. Remember that we get our evidence from sources, and failure to integrate sources into your writing is another major pitfall to avoid. These sources could be textual (like a book) or visual (like a painting) or auditory (like a song). As we've already seen, academics divide all sources into two types: primary and secondary sources. Primary sources give direct access to the subject under study. Secondary sources only provide indirect access. Scholars generally think primary sources provide the best evidence for proving a case. Where do you get these sources so you can find evidence to prove your case? Your professor might give you a source to use. For example, you might read a book in a class and be asked to answer a question dealing with the same topic as the book. In this case, you might use the book as your source to find evidence. Or your professor might ask you to find your own sources. This type of assignment is a research paper. In this case, you get to be a real detective and hunt down sources in the library all by yourself. Or, more likely, you could go to the internet and – hopefully – keep in mind the importance of carefully evaluating sources. In a social science class you might gather sociological data yourself, or in a natural science class you might perform experiments in a laboratory to collect data.

In any case, the body of any argumentative paper should consist of you proving your case point by point, using the order you provided in the blueprint. You do this by providing evidence and explaining how it supports your thesis in each case. Include all the logical steps in your argument. Failure to do so means your reader will not be able to follow your logic. An argument with a missing part is called an enthymeme, which sounds like a rather nasty medical procedure. For example, if you argue that gerrymandering allows politicians to create districts that will ensure their party's continual reelection and, therefore, gerry-mandering endangers democracy, you have produced an enthymeme. *Why* does allowing politicians to craft their own distinct boundar-ies and thereby ensure reelection endanger democracy? Remember, it's never enough to assume your reader can just figure it out on her own. It's your responsibility as a writer to spell out every step in your argument as clearly as possible for readers. You would need to revise your argument as follows: gerrymandering allows politicians to create districts that will ensure their party's continual reelection. The nearly automatic reelection of candidates based on party endangers democ-racy because it limits the choice necessary in a functioning democracy. Therefore, gerrymandering endangers democracy. Throughout your paper, you're guiding your reader along the trail of your argument. To keep them on the path, you'll need to make sure there are no blank spots on the map that leave them stranded. Of course, perfection is not realistic. It's as impossible to never produce a gap in logic as it is to avoid all fallacies that could slip into your writing. Again, fallacies themselves are not errors or mistakes. Rather, they are a means through which we can make mistakes. The important thing is to always be on the lookout for any fallacies in our writing, catch ourselves when we spot them, and then correct ourselves.

In order to let your readers know how they are progressing through your paper, so they can follow your argumentation, each body para-graph should start with a topic sentence that addresses the main point of the whole paragraph. The topic sentence is like the thesis of your paragraph. Then go on to provide evidence to support the mini-argument you made in the topic sentence. You'll also want to avoid fallacies mentioned in the previous chapter, like quote mining and cherry picking. Other fallacies to avoid include using anecdotal evidence based on your own life or experiences as opposed to other sources, unless the assignment calls for the use of anecdotal sources. Speaking of sources, be sure to always cite all of them. Direct quotations, summaries, and paraphrases all need to be cited. Additionally, in humanities and social science papers, you cannot just throw evidence at the reader and expect him to understand how it relates to your thesis. You need to analyze or interpret all evidence. In other words, you need to tell the reader *how* it relates to and supports your thesis.

For example, if you were a defense attorney making an argument to a jury, you wouldn't just say "My client is innocent of this murder charge!," bring out a photograph of blood splatter to show the jury, and then say "I rest my case!" The jury would have no idea how the picture of blood splatter relates to your client being innocent or not. For all they know, the picture could be evidence of your client's guilt. Therefore, the defense attorney needs to *explain* to the jury what the blood splatter evidence means and *how* it demonstrates his client's innocence. This is what you need to do with your evidence in the body paragraphs. Explain what the evidence is and how it supports your argument. Note, though, that you should not attempt to interpret your data in the main body paragraphs of all writing assignments. Be sure to check with your professor if you are unsure. For example, in lab manuscripts you may need to save drawing conclusions for a separate discussion portion of the paper.[3] In any case, in humanities and social science papers, the final sentence in a body paragraph should either summarize the evidence and your analysis of it or explicitly tie the evidence back to the thesis. Ideally, the concluding sentences should show or reiterate how the evidence presented in the paragraph provides warrant (evidentiary justification) for the topic sentence or paper thesis. In other instances, concluding sentences could more simply summarize the paragraph's content. Regardless of how exactly you conclude a body paragraph, don't leave your reader unclear as to the significance of what you have just written.

Within the body of your paper, you'll also be interacting with the ideas of others who have written on your subject. These are the authors of the secondary sources you have consulted or scholars who have gathered relevant primary source data. Understanding that you are part of a larger conversation is part of being a good reader and an important part of academic writing. That's why many research papers and other writing assignments will ask you to explicitly consider what other scholars have written on your topic in a literature review or historiography section of your paper. This could be a separate part of your paper, or you may find yourself discussing how your work compares with that of other scholars throughout your paper. In any case, the key here is to do your best to understand what other authors have said – you should avoid straw men, for example – and then state how your position compares. If necessary, you may also need to consider objections that another author has had or might have to your argument. Respectfully demonstrate, based on evidence, why your interpretation is the best one.

After you finish carefully explaining and analyzing your evidence, you'll need to write a conclusion paragraph or paragraphs. In the natural sciences, this may be called a discussion section. In it, you should restate your thesis or draw conclusions from your data and recap all your main points. Additionally, a strong conclusion will explain the historical or contemporary significance of your argument or subject more generally. Scholars of all types, including scientists, might write here about future avenues for research that their work opens up or any questions still to be answered. But as a rule, you should not bring up entirely new information or ideas in the conclusion.

A few other things to consider about writing humanities papers in particular: when writing a paper for a humanities class, many students are tempted to tell a story. This mode of writing is known as narrative. Unless the assignments calls for it, you should always use narrative sparingly and only to make a point. The goal of many academic papers is not primarily to tell a story, but *to make an argument about your subject*. Therefore, the main mode of writing that you should use is analysis (also called explication). This means you should be answering *how* and *why* questions. Berkin puts it like this: "An analysis looks at different pieces of evidence and presents a thesis. In other words, an analysis proves a point or answers a question. A narrative describes an event, usually in a chronological manner…. Research papers should always be constructed around an analytical framework with narrative sections used only to prove the different points."[4] In *A Short Guide to Writing about History*, Richard Marius describes analysis, which he calls "exposition," like this: "expositions explain and analyze – philosophical ideas, causes of events, the significance of decisions, the motives of participants, the working of an organization, the ideology of a political party. Any time you set out to explain cause and effect, or the meaning of an event or an idea, you write in expository [analytical] mode."[5]

What if I'm Not Writing a History Paper?

So far we've been using the example of writing a research-style paper for a history class on the English Civil War. You may think that the types of writing assignments you will have in other disciplines are too far afield for any of this to be relevant. That's actually not the case. Many, if not most, formal academic writing assignments have similar elements. Suppose you are writing that lab manuscript to which we've alluded for a biology class. Do you still need to include many of the same elements we've already discussed? The answer is a resounding yes. Biologists also select subjects, ask questions, and provide answers or findings. These generally appear within an introductory section. Lab manuscripts in upper-level courses may also include the functional equivalent of a literature review by informing the reader of any other scientists who have studied the same question. The middle section of lab manuscripts explains methodology, something you should also do in humanities and social science papers, and presents data for scrutiny. Interpretation of data and exploration of its significance, however, happens in the discussion section, which is similar to the conclusion of other types of papers.[6]

Style

One final thing to consider is the need to develop a clear and concise style of writing. Even in an age of spelling and grammar checkers, the ability to express your meaning to readers remains important. In fact, the primary function of clear writing and grammar is not to trip you up and lower your grades but to help you think clearly and convey

your ideas to others.[7] I often find that first- and second-year undergraduate students are eager to impress their professors and peers. As a
result, they slide into writing that inadvertently uses showy or affected
language that is often not employed correctly. As you may be able to
guess at this point, the result is that they sometimes accidentally slide
into pseudo-profundity.

If this has happened to you, take courage and write like yourself,
not the way you think your writing should sound. In other words, in
the first draft at least, write down the words the way they naturally
come to you in your mind. In the past I have asked students to read
particularly difficult-to-comprehend sentences that they've written and
then asked them if they would ever speak like that out loud. If the
answer is no, and it always is, then I tell them that there's simply no
need to torture yourself trying to write in that style. It's not yours. I
then ask them to rephrase for me what they had written the way they
would speak it aloud to me. The result is always clear and understandable. I then advise them to write that instead. One caveat I always add,
however, is that we do shift registers, meaning we do not speak the
same way in every situation. So you might speak differently with your
friends at an informal gathering than you would at a job interview.
So there remains a range of speech or language that a given individual would use. I advise students to "speak"/write in papers as though
they were in a professional environment, which of course they are.

By now we've discussed some of the obstacles preventing all of us, not
only students, from knowing fact from fiction, truth from falsehood.
The democratization of knowledge brought about by the internet has
opened up many new avenues through which we can receive information. The democratization of access to information has opened up
new opportunities for historically marginalized groups and allowed
new and more diverse voices to be heard. But it has also pushed aside
the old institutional gatekeepers that – albeit imperfectly – attempted
to filter out falsehoods like fake news and fallacies. It's up to us now to
take a humble but active approach to discerning truth from falsehood.
Humble, because we don't automatically know everything and can
make mistakes when we attempt to act in isolation as our own gatekeepers. In a twenty-four-hour news cycle, this may mean waiting a
few days while journalists and professional fact-checkers get the facts

straight before you pass judgment. Remember the 2019 viral video featuring an apparently smirking Covington Catholic High School student standing face to face with Native American activist Nathan Phillips? In their rush to attract readers, even established media outlets jumped the gun before the facts were fully known. Inadvertently misleading stories indicated that the Covington students had incited a dispute with a Native American group present in Washington, DC, for the Indigenous Peoples March. Further investigation showed that the situation was considerably more complex and also involved a third group consisting of Black Hebrew Israelites. As a result, the initial portrayal of the Covington Catholic students was largely inaccurate. Student Nicholas Sandmann responded by filing defamation lawsuits against the *Washington Post*, CNN, and NBC.[8]

As this example illustrates, we need to avoid jumping to conclusions by taking time to process information. A crucial element of this approach is actively interrogating the sources we read, both print and electronic. This includes books, newspapers, texts, tweets, and (especially) memes. Even if the sources themselves pass the CRAAP test and appear reliable, we need to read them analytically. Part of this process is being alert to the types of common formal and informal fallacies highlighted in chapters 6, 7, and 8. Finally, having filtered out the facts from the errors and distinguished between likely interpretations and mere opinions, it's time for you to join the wider civic discourse yourself. You'll do this in spoken communication, of course, but also via writing, which teaches you how to clarify and express your thoughts in service of the truth. I hope this book has helped equip you for this task.

NOTES

Chapter 1: Introduction

1 "Fake News of 2017," Information is Beautiful, accessed December 30, 2017, https://informationisbeautiful.net/visualizations/biggest -fake-news-of-2017/.

2 Joshua Gillin, "NFL's Goodell Didn't Say He Would Fine Steelers Players $1 Million Each for Skipping National Anthem," PolitiFact, Poynter Institute, September 25, 2017, http://www.politifact.com/punditfact /statements/2017/sep/25/thelastlineofdefenseorg/nfls-goodell-didnt-say -he-would-fine-steelers-play/; Alex Huntley, "Palestinians Recognize Texas as Part of Mexico," Beaverton, December 6, 2017, https://www .thebeaverton.com/2017/12/palestinians-recognize-texas-part-mexico/.

3 Joshua Gillin, "If You're Fooled by Fake News, This Man Probably Wrote It," PolitiFact, Poynter Institute, May 31, 2017, http://www.politifact.com /punditfact/article/2017/may/31/If-youre-fooled-by-fake-news-this -man-probably-wro/.

4 Some researchers define the Post-Millennial Generation as those born between 1999 and 2015.

5 See Jonathan Alger and Mark Piper, "Administration, Faculty, and the Hard Free-Speech Questions," *Academe* 105, no. 1 (Winter 2019): 14–19; and Michel C. Behrent, "A Tale of Two Arguments about Free Speech on Campus," *Academe* 105, no. 1 (Winter 2019): 31–5.

6 See Wineburg et al., "Evaluating Information," 23–4.

7 Maloy and Malinowski, *Wiki Works*, 38; Kristen Purcell, Judy Buchanan, and Linda Friedrich, "How Teachers Are Using Technology at Home and in Their Classrooms," Pew Research Center, February 28, 2013, https://www.pewresearch.org/internet/2013/02/28 /how-teachers-are-using-technology-at-home-and-in-their-classrooms/.

8 "Advocacy for Liberal Education," Association of American Colleges and Universities, accessed June 1, 2018, https://www.aacu.org/leap /what-is-a-liberal-education.

9   "Advocacy for Liberal Education."

10   Ellen Wayland-Smith, "Commentary: Where Do Students Learn about Fake News? In Freshman Comp," *Chronicle of Higher Education*, February 26, 2017, https://www.chronicle.com/article/Commentary-Where-Do -Students/239266.

11   Colleen Flaherty, "'A Different Kind of University,'" Inside Higher Ed, March 13, 2018, https://www.insidehighered.com/news/2018/03/13 /faculty-members-wisconsin-stevens-point-react-plan-cut-13-majors. The plan to cut these thirteen majors led to enough pushback that the university reversed course and eventually decided to retain them after all. See Colleen Flaherty, "Cuts Reversed at Stevens Point," Inside Higher Ed, April 11, 2019, https://www.insidehighered.com/news/2019/04/11 /stevens-point-abandons-controversial-plan-cut-liberal-arts-majors -including-history.

12   Scott Jaschik, "Shocker: Humanities Grads Gainfully Employed and Happy," Inside Higher Ed, February 7, 2018, https://www.insidehighered .com/news/2018/02/07/study-finds-humanities-majors-land-jobs-and -are-happy-them; *The State of the Humanities 2018: Graduates in the Workforce and Beyond*, Humanities Indicators (Cambridge, MA: American Academy of Arts & Sciences, 2018), https://www.amacad.org/multimedia/pdfs /publications/researchpapersmonographs/HI_Workforce-2018.pdf; Jeffrey Dorfman, "Surprise: Humanities Degrees Provide Great Return on Investment," *Forbes*, November 20, 2014, https://www.forbes.com/sites /jeffreydorfman/2014/11/20/surprise-humanities-degrees-provide -great-return-on-investment; Derek Newton, "It's Not Liberal Arts and Literature Majors Who Are Most Underemployed," *Forbes*, May 31, 2018, https://www.forbes.com/sites/dereknewton/2018/05/31 /its-not-liberal-arts-and-literature-majors-who-are-most-underemployed.

13   Quoted in Scott Jaschik, "In Defense of the Liberal Arts," Insider Higher Ed, June 1, 2018, https://www.insidehighered.com/news/2018/06/01 /two-groups-whose-memberships-extend-beyond-liberal-arts-issue -statement-support.

14   Raab, *Who Is the Historian?*, 90.

15   Fischer, *Historians' Fallacies*, xvii.

16   See David Gooblar, "How to Teach Information Literacy in an Era of Lies," *Chronicle of Higher Education*, July 24, 2018, https://www.chronicle .com/article/How-to-Teach-Information/243973.

Chapter 2: You're in College, But You Don't Know Everything

1   George Anders, "Good News Liberal-Arts Majors: Your Peers Probably Won't Outearn You Forever," *Wall Street Journal*, September 11, 2016,

https://www.wsj.com/articles/good-news-liberal-arts-majors
-your-peers-probably-wont-outearn-you-forever-1473645902. See
also Randall Stross, *A Practical Education: Why Liberal Arts Majors
Make Great Employees* (Stanford: Stanford University Press, 2017);
Scott Hartley, *The Fuzzy and the Techie: Why the Liberal Arts Will
Rule the Digital World* (Boston: Houghton Mifflin Harcourt, 2017);
George Anders, "That 'Useless' Liberal Arts Degree Has Become
Tech's Hottest Ticket," *Forbes*, July 29, 2015, https://www.forbes
.com/sites/georgeanders/2015/07/29/liberal-arts-degree-tech; and
Willard Dix, "A Liberal Arts Degree Is More Important Than
Ever," *Forbes*, November 16, 2016, https://www.forbes.com/sites
/willarddix/2016/11/16/a-liberal-arts-degree-is-more-important-than-ever.

2 E. Koc and A. Koncz, *Job Outlook 2010* (Bethlehem, PA: National
Association of Colleges and Employers, 2009), 15, 24. See also Roche,
Liberal Arts, 13.

3 Roche, *Liberal Arts*, 60. See also Koc and Koncz, *Job Outlook 2010*, 23.

4 Joan W. Scott, "Academic Freedom and Free Speech on Campus,"
interview by Bill Moyers, *Academe* 104, no. 1 (January–February 2018): 21.

5 Postman, *Technopoly*, 4–5.

6 Amy Mitchell, Jeffrey Gottfried, Sophia Fedeli, Galen Stocking, and
Mason Walker, "Many Americans Say Made-Up News Is a Critical
Problem That Needs to Be Fixed," Pew Research Center, June 5, 2019,
https://www.journalism.org/2019/06/05/many-americans-say-made-up
-news-is-a-critical-problem-that-needs-to-be-fixed/.

7 Ball, *Post-Truth*, 145.

8 Ball, *Post-Truth*, 147.

9 Elisa Shearer and Katerina Eva Matsa, "News Use across Social Media
Platforms 2018," Pew Research Center, September 10, 2018, http://www
.journalism.org/2018/09/10/news-use-across-social-media-platforms
-2018/.

10 Shearer and Matsa, "News Use"; Elisa Shearer and Jeffrey Gottfried,
"News Use across Social Media Platforms 2017," Pew Research Center,
September 7, 2017, http://www.journalism.org/2017/09/07/news-use
-across-social-media-platforms-2017/.

11 Elisa Shearer, "Social Media Outpaces Print Newspapers in the U.S.
as a News Source," Fact Tank, Pew Research Center, December 10,
2018, http://www.pewresearch.org/fact-tank/2018/12/10
/social-media-outpaces-print-newspapers-in-the-u-s-as-a-news-source.

12 Craig Silverman, "I Helped Popularize the Term 'Fake News'
and Now I Cringe Every Time I Hear It," BuzzFeed News,
December 31, 2017, https://www.buzzfeednews.com/article

/craigsilverman/i-helped-popularize-the-term-fake-news-and-now-i
-cringe.

13 Silverman, "I Helped Popularize."

14 Juju Chang, Jake Lefferman, Claire Pedersen, and Geoff Martz,
"When Fake News Stories Make Real News Headlines," ABC
News, November 29, 2016, https://abcnews.go.com/Technology
/fake-news-stories-make-real-news-headlines/story?id=43845383.

15 Shearer and Matsa, "News Use."

16 Craig Silverman and Lawrence Alexander, "How Teens in the Balkans Are
Duping Trump Supporters with Fake News," BuzzFeed News, November 3,
2016, https://www.buzzfeednews.com/article/craigsilverman/how
-macedonia-became-a-global-hub-for-pro-trump-misinfo.

17 Chang et al., "Fake News Stories."

18 Ball, Post-Truth, 151.

19 Quoted in Chang et al., "Fake News Stories." See Ball, Post-Truth, 138–9.

20 Pariser, Filter Bubble.

21 R. Hobbs, "President Trump Orders the Execution of Five Turkeys
Pardoned by Obama," Real News Right Now, January 24, 2017, http://
realnewsrightnow.com/2017/01/president-trump-orders-execution
-five-turkeys-pardoned-obama/.

22 Ball, Post-Truth, 154–7.

23 Maloy and Malinowski, Wiki Works, 35.

24 Soroush Vosoughi, Deb Roy, and Sinan Aral, "The Spread of True and
False News Online," Science 359, no. 6380 (March 9, 2018): 1146–51. See
also Robinson Meyer, "The Grim Conclusions of the Largest-Ever Study
of Fake News," Atlantic, March 8, 2018, https://www.theatlantic.com
/technology/archive/2018/03/largest-study-ever-fake-news-mit-twitter
/555104/.

25 Quoted in Meyer, "Grim Conclusions."

26 Craig Silverman, Jane Lytvynenko, and Scott Pham, "These Are 50 of
the Biggest Fake News Hits on Facebook in 2017," BuzzFeed News,
December 28, 2017, https://www.buzzfeed.com/craigsilverman
/these-are-50-of-the-biggest-fake-news-hits-on-facebook-in.

27 Meyer, "Grim Conclusions."

28 Quoted in Meyer, "Grim Conclusions"; emphasis in original.

29 "Momo Challenge: The Anatomy of a Hoax," BBC News, February 28,
2019, https://www.bbc.com/news/technology-47393510.

30 Silverman, "I Helped Popularize."

31 Amy Mitchell, Jeffrey Gottfried, Elisa Shearer, and Kristine Lu, "How
Americans Encounter, Recall and Act Upon Digital News," Pew Research
Center, February 9, 2017, http://www.journalism.org/2017/02/09
/how-americans-encounter-recall-and-act-upon-digital-news/.

32 Mitchell et al., "Digital News."

33 Mitchell et al., "Digital News," 4; emphasis in original.

34 Wineburg et al., "Evaluating Information," 6.

35 Wineburg et al., "Evaluating Information," 10.

36 Wineburg et al., "Evaluating Information," 17.

37 Wineburg et al., "Evaluating Information," 23.

38 For a list of other studies, see Maloy and Malinowski, *Wiki Works*, 36.

39 Sue Shellenbarger, "Most Students Don't Know When News Is Fake, Stanford Study Finds," *Wall Street Journal*, November 21, 2016, http:// www.wsj.com/articles/most-students-dont-know-when-news-is-fake -stanford-study-finds-1479752576.

40 Wineburg et al., "Evaluating Information," 5.

41 Wineburg, "Historical Thinking," 14.

42 Wineburg, "Historical Thinking," 16.

43 Donald J. Trump, "A very big part of the Anger we see today...," Twitter, October 25, 2018, 4:18 a.m., https://twitter.com/realDonaldTrump/ status/1055418269270716418.

44 See Brendan Brown, Trump Twitter Archive, accessed May 17, 2019, http://trumptwitterarchive.com/; and Amanda Wills and Alysha Love, "All the President's Tweets," CNN, last updated November 7, 2019, https:// www.cnn.com/interactive/2017/politics/trump-tweets/. Brown explains the process of gathering tweets at "Getting All the Tweets," accessed October 8, 2020, http://trumptwitterarchive.com/howto/all_tweets.html.

Chapter 3: Evaluating Statements and Identifying Sources

1 I'm using the definition that the Pew Research Center uses in its 2018 study: see Amy Mitchell, Jeffrey Gottfried, Michael Barthel, and Nami Sumida, "Distinguishing between Factual and Opinion Statements in the News," Pew Research Center, June 18, 2018, http://www.journalism .org/2018/06/18/distinguishing-between-factual-and-opinion-statements -in-the-news/. Note that some theorists, like Kevin Passmore, define a fact as a statement that is true by definition. Passmore, "Evidence and Interpretation," 141.

2 Note that postmodern thinkers may talk about "facts" differently. Later in your college career you may encounter other ways of thinking about facts, objectivity, and subjectivity.

3 See Passmore, "Evidence and Interpretation," 140–2.

4 Mitchell et al., "Factual and Opinion Statements."

5 Mitchell et al., "Factual and Opinion Statements."

6 Mitchell et al., "Factual and Opinion Statements."

7 Again, for the definitions I'm using, see Mitchell et al., "Factual and Opinion Statements."

8   Passmore, "Evidence and Interpretation," 140; emphasis in original.

9   Passmore, "Evidence and Interpretation," 142.

10   Passmore, "Evidence and Interpretation," 144.

11   "Whose Heritage? Public Symbols of the Confederacy," Southern Poverty Law Center, February 1, 2019, https://www.splcenter.org/20190201 /whose-heritage-public-symbols-confederacy.

12   Luke E. Taylor, Amy L. Swerdfeger, and Guy D. Eslick, "Vaccines Are Not Associated with Autism: An Evidence-Based Meta-Analysis of Case-Control and Cohort Studies," *Vaccine* 32, no. 29 (June 17, 2014): 3623, https://doi.org/10.1016/j.vaccine.2014.04.085.

13   Associated Press, "A Timeline of the US Involvement in Syria's Conflict," *AP News*, January 11, 2019, https://www.apnews.com/967012254c5a448c b253f14ab697419b.

14   Arnold, *History*, 13.

15   Passmore, "Evidence and Interpretation," 143.

16   Passmore, "Evidence and Interpretation," 139.

17   Trueman, *Histories and Fallacies*, 27, 63, 66.

18   Novick, *That Noble Dream*.

19   Trueman, *Histories and Fallacies*, 21, 27–9.

20   Trueman, *Histories and Fallacies*, 21, 28.

21   Trueman, *Histories and Fallacies*, 28–9.

22   Let me pause here to say that, yes, some postmodern philosophers and other scholars will argue that unimpeded access to *anything* is impossible. At this point in your education, let's just set that conjecture aside and leave it as an intriguing possibility for you to ponder as you continue in your education. For more on primary and secondary sources, see Presnell, *Information-Literate Historian*, 52–3, 109.

23   Presnell, *Information-Literate Historian*, 6, 109.

24   Thanks to student reviewer Nalana La Framboise for her insights here on the connection to coaching.

25   See "Distinguishing Scholarly Articles," Meriam Library, California State University, Chico, August 2011, https://library.csuchico.edu/sites/default /files/scholarly.pdf.

26   Note that many authors ask readers not to cite or circulate unpublished material without permission. Be sure to check any unpublished papers you read on Academia.edu (https://www.academia.edu/) or elsewhere for these restrictions.

27   See, for example, "Distinguish between Primary and Secondary Sources," University Library, UC Santa Cruz, accessed March 25, 2019, https:// guides.library.ucsc.edu/primarysecondary; and Susan Thomas, "Basic Differences," Borough of Manhattan Community College Library, accessed October 8, 2020, https://bmcc.libguides.com/primarysecondary.

28   Jordanova, *History in Practice*, 38.

Chapter 4: Evaluating Sources with the CRAAP Test

1 See Eszter Hargittai, Lindsay Fullerton, Ericka Menchen-Trevino, and Kristin Yates Thomas, "Trust Online: Young Adults' Evaluation of Web Content," *International Journal of Communication* 4 (2010): 468–94, cited in Wineburg, "Historical Thinking," 15.

2 "Evaluating Information – Applying the CRAAP Test," Meriam Library, California State University, Chico, September 17, 2010, https://library .csuchico.edu/sites/default/files/craap-test.pdf; "The CRAAP Test," Meriam Library, California State University, Chico, December 11, 2018, http://libguides.csuchico.edu/LiteratureReviews?p=2822716.

3 Anisa Subedar, "Why Is Leslie Nielsen STILL Dead?," *BBC Trending* (blog), BBC News, January 20, 2016, https://www.bbc.com/news /blogs-trending-35363394.

4 "About the Internet Archive," Internet Archive, accessed January 15, 2019, https://archive.org/about/. See also Raab, *Who Is the Historian?*, 86.

5 However, as the Internet Archive notes, the last page archived may not always be the most recent version of a page because the archive crawler may not have accessed that version.

6 Maddie Crum, "After Trump Was Elected, Librarians Had to Rethink Their System for Fact-Checking," HuffPost, April 18, 2017, https://www .huffingtonpost.com/entry/after-trump-librarians-develop-new-fact -checking-system_us_58c071d3e4b0ed7182699786.

7 David Mikkelson, "FBI Agent Suspected in Hillary Email Leaks Found Dead in Apparent Murder-Suicide," Snopes, accessed March 25, 2019, https://www.snopes.com/fact-check/fbi-agent-murder-suicide/.

8 "Website Research: URLs," University Libraries, Central Michigan University, updated July 10, 2020, https://libguides.cmich.edu/web _research/urls; Presnell, *Information-Literate Historian*, 168.

9 Bobby Allyn, "Researchers: Nearly Half of Accounts Tweeting about Coronavirus Are Likely Bots," NPR, May 20, 2020, https://www.npr.org /sections/coronavirus-live-updates/2020/05/20/859814085/researchers -nearly-half-of-accounts-tweeting-about-coronavirus-are-likely -bots.

10 Will Knight, "How to Tell If You're Talking to a Bot," *MIT Technology Review*, July 18, 2018, https://www.technologyreview.com/s/611655 /how-to-tell-if-youre-talking-to-a-bot/.

11 Andy Borowitz, "DeVos Says Trump's Forty-Per-Cent Approval Rating Means More Than Half of Country Supports Him," *New Yorker*, February 13, 2017, https://www.newyorker.com/humor/borowitz-report/devos -says-trumps-forty-per-cent-approval-rating-means-more-than-half-of -country-supports-him.

12 "Fake News of 2017," Information Is Beautiful.

13 David Gooblar, "How to Teach Information Literacy in an Era of Lies," *Chronicle of Higher Education*, July 24, 2018, https://www.chronicle.com /article/How-to-Teach-Information/243973.

14 Michael Caulfield, "How 'News Literacy' Gets the Web Wrong," *Hapgood* (blog), March 4, 2017, https://hapgood.us/2017/03/04/how-news -literacy-gets-the-web-wrong/. Caulfield is also director of blended and networked learning at Washington State University Vancouver.

15 Robert Harris, "Evaluating Internet Research Sources," VirtualSalt, last modified October 11, 2018, https://www.virtualsalt.com/evalu8it.htm; emphasis in original.

16 Caulfield, "'News Literacy.'"

17 "Fact Checking & Verification for Reporting: Fact-Checking Your Reporting," Craig Newmark Graduate School of Journalism at the City University of New York, last updated August 25, 2020, https://researchguides.journalism. cuny.edu/c.php?g=547454&p=4256107; "Evaluating Information," American Library Association, March 18, 2019, http://libguides.ala.org /InformationEvaluation. See also Cooke, *Fake News and Alternative Facts*.

18 Angelo Fichera, "Social Media Posts Make Baseless Claim on COVID-19 Death Toll," FactCheck.org, April 8, 2020, https://www.factcheck.org /2020/04/social-media-posts-make-baseless-claim-on-covid-19 -death-toll/.

19 Jessica McDonald, "COVID-19 Face Mask Advice, Explained," FactCheck.org, April 6, 2020, https://www.factcheck.org/2020/04 /covid-19-face-mask-advice-explained/.

20 Jessica McDonald, "Baseless Conspiracy Theories Claim New Coronavirus Was Bioengineered," FactCheck.org, February 7, 2020, https://www .factcheck.org/2020/02/baseless-conspiracy-theories-claim-new -coronavirus-was-bioengineered/. See also Angelo Fichera, Saranac Hale Spencer, D'Angelo Gore, Lori Robertson, and Eugene Kiely, "The Falsehoods of the 'Plandemic' Video," FactCheck.org, May 8, 2020, https:// www.factcheck.org/2020/05/the-falsehoods-of-the-plandemic-video/.

21 Angelo Fichera, "No Evidence That Flu Shot Increases Risk of COVID- 19," FactCheck.org, April 27, 2020, https://www.factcheck.org/2020/04 /no-evidence-that-flu-shot-increases-risk-of-covid-19/. See also Fichera et al., "Falsehoods of the 'Plandemic' Video."

22 "About," Event 201: A Global Pandemic Exercise, accessed May 13, 2020, https://www.centerforhealthsecurity.org/event201/about.

23 Angelo Fichera, "New Coronavirus Wasn't 'Predicted' in Simulation," FactCheck.org, January 29, 2020, https://www.factcheck.org/2020/01 /new-coronavirus-wasnt-predicted-in-simulation/.

24 Harris, "Evaluating Internet Research Sources."

25 "Interactive Media Bias Chart," Ad Fontes Media, accessed April 10, 2019, https://www.adfontesmedia.com/interactive-media-bias-chart-2/.

26 "Chart History," Ad Fontes Media, accessed October 8, 2020, https://
    www.adfontesmedia.com/evolution-of-the-media-bias-chart/; "The
    Media Bias Chart: Version 6.0," Ad Fontes Media, accessed October 8,
    2020, https://www.adfontesmedia.com/intro-to-the-media-bias-chart/.

27 [Vanessa Otero], "Founder's Political Biases," Ad Fontes Media, accessed
    June 26, 2019, https://www.adfontesmedia.com/who-am-i-and-what
    -are-my-political-biases/.

28 "About Us," AllSides website, accessed June 26, 2019, https://www.allsides
    .com/about.

29 "AllSides Media Bias Chart," AllSides website, accessed June 26, 2019,
    https://www.allsides.com/media-bias/media-bias-chart.

30 "Website Research: URLs," University Libraries, Central Michigan
    University, last updated August 26, 2020, https://libguides.cmich.edu
    /web_research/urls. See also "Evaluating Websites," Camden-Carroll
    Library, Morehead State University, last updated December 13, 2018,
    https://research.moreheadstate.edu/evaluatingwebsites/urls.

31 "Evaluating Websites," Camden-Carroll Library, Morehead State University.

32 Kelly, *Teaching History*, 40.

33 Wineburg, "Historical Thinking," 16.

34 Kelly, *Teaching History*, 43–5; Raab, *Who Is the Historian?*, 86.

35 Kelly, *Teaching History*, 42–3.

36 Gula, *Nonsense*, 35–9.

37 Daniel Marans, "Donald Trump's Political Arm Cites InfoWars in an Email
    Boasting about Crowd Size," HuffPost, June 3, 2017, https://www.huffpost.com
    /entry/alex-jones-donald-trump-fundraising-email_n_593306d1e4b0c242ca249805.

38 "Adam Mill [pseud.], "7 Reasons 2019 Is Already a Terrible Year for
    Trump's Opponents," Federalist, March 4, 2019, https://thefederalist
    .com/2019/03/04/7-reasons-2019-already-terrible-year-trumps-opponents/.

39 A handy chart called "Evaluating Resources using the 'CRAAP Test'" is
    available at "Evaluating Sources: Evaluation Criteria," Hekman Library
    Research Guides, Calvin University, last updated June 23, 2020, http://
    libguides.calvin.edu/evaluating/criteria.

40 "Daniel Marans," HuffPost, accessed October 8, 2020, https://www
    .huffpost.com/author/daniel-marans.

41 "Adam Mill," Federalist, accessed October 8, 2020, https://thefederalist
    .com/author/adammill/.

Chapter 5: Reading Your Sources

1   I am indebted to Julie Bevins, the Writing Center coordinator at Aquinas
    College, for the idea of textual houses with room and conversations.

2   See Victoria Clayton, "The Needless Complexity of Academic Writing,"
    Atlantic, October 26, 2015, https://www.theatlantic.com/education
    /archive/2015/10/complex-academic-writing/412255/.

3   Heather Cox Richardson, "Richardson's Rules of Order, Part IV: How to Read for a College History Course," *The Historical Society: A Blog Devoted to History for the Academy & Beyond*, May 28, 2009, http://histsociety .blogspot.com/2009/05/richardsons-rules-of-order-part-iv-how.html.

4   See "How to Read for History," W. Caleb McDaniel website, August 1, 2008, http://wcm1.web.rice.edu/howtoread.html.

5   Patrick French, *Liberty or Death: India's Journey to Independence and Division* (London: Flamingo, 1998).

6   For more information about writing précis, see Rampolla, *Pocket Guide*, 29, 38–9.

7   See Rampolla, *Pocket Guide*, 38.

8   Rampolla, *Pocket Guide*, 39.

9   Mary Lynn Rampolla must have had similar experiences. See Rampolla, *Pocket Guide*, 38–9.

10   For more information on asking analytical questions and not writing in the first person, see Rampolla, *Pocket Guide*, 38–9.

11   Rampolla, *Pocket Guide*, 29.

12   Rampolla, *Pocket Guide*, 29.

13   Bethany Kilcrease, "Radical Anti-Catholic Protestantism and *When It Was Dark*: The Novel and the Historical Context," *English Literature in Transition, 1880–1920* 57, no. 2 (January 2014): 210.

14   Bethany Kilcrease, "Working for the Common Good through Worldview Encounters: An Application in Teaching the Reformation at Catholic Colleges," *Journal of Catholic Higher Education* 37, no. 2 (Summer 2018): 219–20.

Chapter 6: Evaluating the Content of Sources – Fallacies of Causation

1   See Van Vleet, *Informal Logical Fallacies*, ix–x.

2   Gula, *Nonsense*, 46; emphasis in original.

3   See Hurley, *Concise Introduction*, 41.

4   Gula, *Nonsense*, 46–7. See also Hurley, *Concise Introduction*, 44.

5   For more on formal versus informal fallacies, see Van Vleet, *Informal Logical Fallacies*, ix–x; and Gula, *Nonsense*, 46–53.

6   See Hurley, *Concise Introduction*, 110.

7   Van Vleet, *Informal Logical Fallacies*, ix. On informal logic as a discipline, see also Walton, *Informal Fallacies*, chap. 11.

8   I've borrowed groupings from Blique, *Logical Fallacy Monsters*; Gula, *Nonsense*; Van Vleet, *Informal Logical Fallacies*; and Fischer, *Historians' Fallacies*.

9   Blique, *Logical Fallacy Monsters*, 6–7; Gula, *Nonsense*, 60.

10   See Gula's "Pepomint" example in *Nonsense*, 60.

11   Blique, *Logical Fallacy Monsters*, 8; Van Vleet, *Informal Logical Fallacies*, 36.

12   Blique, *Logical Fallacy Monsters*, 9.

13   Blique, *Logical Fallacy Monsters*, 10–11.

14 Fea, *Why Study History?*, 6. The "five Cs" originally come from Thomas Andrews and Flannery Burke, "What Does It Mean to Think Historically?," *AHA Perspectives* (January 2007), https://www.historians.org/publications-and-directories/perspectives-on-history/january-2007/what-does-it-mean-to-think-historically.

15 You could also argue in this example that setting the class time and not showing up together constituted the direct primary cause of tardiness.

16 See William Bechtel, "Causal Explanation" (PowerPoint slides, Philosophy 12, University of California San Diego, Winter 2005), http://mechanism.ucsd.edu/teaching/phil12/lectures/Causalexplanation.pdf.

17 Gaddis, *Landscape of History*, chap. 6.

18 Bloch's example comes via Gaddis, *Landscape of History*, 94–8.

19 See Trueman, *Histories and Fallacies*, 152–6; Fischer, *Historians' Fallacies*, 166–7; and Marius and Page, *Short Guide*, 40–1.

20 See Trueman's "socialism" example. Trueman, *Histories and Fallacies*, 142–4.

21 Some idealist or poststructuralist philosophers might debate this point on a variety of different levels, but in general, especially at the undergraduate level, this is an important rule of thumb.

Chapter 7: Fallacies of Narration, Generalization, and Evidence

1 For more information, see Fischer, *Historians' Fallacies*, 132–5. See also Trueman, *Histories and Fallacies*, chap. 3.

2 Blique, *Logical Fallacy Monsters*, 102–3.

3 Fischer, *Historians' Fallacies*, 104–5.

4 See Trueman, *Histories and Fallacies*, 160–2.

5 Fischer, *Historians' Fallacies*, 109.

6 Gaddis, *Landscape of History*, 63.

7 Blique, *Logical Fallacy Monsters*, 76–7.

8 Gula, *Nonsense*, 122–3; Blique, *Logical Fallacy Monsters*, 79.

9 Gula, *Nonsense*, 125.

10 See Trueman, *Histories and Fallacies*, 146–52; and Marius and Page, *Short Guide*, 41.

11 Fischer, *Historians' Fallacies*, 172. On oversimplified causation, see also Gaddis, *Landscape of History*, 64–5.

12 Gaddis, *Landscape of History*, 64–5.

13 Gula, *Nonsense*, 25.

14 Chaffee, *Thinking Critically*, 456.

15 Gula, *Nonsense*, 141.

16 See Fischer, *Historians' Fallacies*, chap. 2.

17 Fischer, *Historians' Fallacies*, 47.

18 Fischer, *Historians' Fallacies*, 63.

19 Van Vleet, *Informal Logical Fallacies*, 12–13.

20 Fischer, *Historians' Fallacies*, 45–7.

21 Ball, *Post-Truth*, 184.

22 Gula, *Nonsense*, 71–5.

23 Oscar Rousseau, "How Many Hot Dogs Do Americans Eat?,"
    FoodNavigator-USA, April 5, 2017, https://www.foodnavigator-usa.com
    /Article/2017/04/06/How-many-hot-dogs-do-Americans-eat.

24 See Gula, *Nonsense*, 72–5.

Chapter 8: Fallacies of Diversion

1   I take this term from Jacob Van Vleet, who refers to some of what follows as
    fallacies of "intrusion," although he groups others in different categories.
    See Van Vleet, *Informal Logical Fallacies*, chap. 3.

2   Blique, *Logical Fallacy Monsters*, 20–1.

3   Gula, *Nonsense*, 80–1.

4   Gula, *Nonsense*, 59.

5   Trueman, *Histories and Fallacies*, 158.

6   See also Fischer, *Historians' Fallacies*, 155.

7   Gula, *Nonsense*, 66.

8   "Founding Fathers Quotes: Quotes about Liberty and Freedom from
    America's Revolutionaries," Ammo.com, accessed June 24, 2019, https://
    ammo.com/articles/founding-fathers-quotes. See also the second search
    result, "Founding Fathers – Top 25 Quotes," Founding Father Quotes,
    accessed October 8, 2020, http://www.foundingfatherquotes.com/quotes
    _top.php/.

9   Gula, *Nonsense*, 66.

10 Gula, *Nonsense*, 67–8.

11 See Marius and Page, *Short Guide*, 39–40.

12 Gula, *Nonsense*, 87–8.

13 Lev. 16:21 ESV.

14 Van Vleet, *Informal Logical Fallacies*, 16; Walton, *Informal Fallacies*, 217–22.

15 See Walton, *Informal Fallacies*, 218.

16 See Robinson Meyer, "The Grim Conclusions of the Largest-Ever
    Study of Fake News," *Atlantic*, March 8, 2018, https://www.theatlantic
    .com/technology/archive/2018/03/largest-study-ever-fake-news-mit-twitter
    /555104/.

17 Samantha Lefave, "Sarah McLachlan Reveals the Truth about Those Sad
    ASPCA Ads," *Redbook*, January 4, 2016, https://www.redbookmag.com
    /life/pets/news/a41805/sarah-mclachlan-aspca-commercial/.

18 "About Us," American Society for the Prevention of Cruelty to Animals,
    accessed July 11, 2018, https://www.aspca.org/about-us.

19 Gula, *Nonsense*, 9.

20 Robert P. George and Cornel West, "Truth Seeking, Democracy, and
    Freedom of Thought and Expression," James Madison Program in
    American Ideals and Institutions, Princeton University, March 14, 2017,
    https://jmp.princeton.edu/statement.

21 Quoted in Maloy and Malinowski, *Wiki Works*, 36. See Steven Cherry, "Don't Believe Everything You See on the Internet," IEEE Spectrum, February 22, 2011, https://spectrum.ieee.org/podcast/at-work/education /do-you-believe-this-headline.

22 See Trueman, *Histories and Fallacies*, 45–52.

23 Gula, *Nonsense*, 281; Van Vleet, *Informal Logical Fallacies*, 20. A version of this fallacy is also sometimes called the *fallacy of the prevalent proof*. See Fischer, *Historians' Fallacies*, 51–3.

24 See Marius and Page, *Short Guide*, 39.

25 Gilbert K. Chesterton, *Orthodoxy* (London: John Lane, 1908), 85.

26 Biblehub, s.v. "pharmakeia," accessed February 17, 2019, https://biblehub .com/greek/5331.htm.

27 Trueman, *Histories and Fallacies*, 156.

28 See Trueman, *Histories and Fallacies*, 156.

29 Quoted in Victoria Clayton, "The Needless Complexity of Academic Writing," *Atlantic*, October 26, 2015, https://www.theatlantic.com /education/archive/2015/10/complex-academic-writing/412255/.

30 This is a version of the example "I am opposed to taxes which slow economic growth," from Austin Cline, "Fallacy of Amphiboly," Learn Religions, August 27, 2018, https://www.learnreligions.com /fallacy-of-amphiboly-250326.

31 Blique, *Logical Fallacy Monsters*, 58–9.

32 Thomas Jefferson to William Stephens Smith, November 13, 1787, *Founders Online*, National Archives, accessed April 29, 2019, http://founders .archives.gov/documents/Jefferson/01-12-02-0348.

33 Jefferson to Smith, November 13, 1787.

34 Van Vleet, *Informal Logical Fallacies*, 3.

35 Trueman, *Histories and Fallacies*, 164.

36 American Civil Liberties Union, "Interested Persons Memo on Crack/ Powder Cocaine Sentencing Policy," May 21, 2002, https://www.aclu.org /other/interested-persons-memo-crackpowder-cocaine-sentencing -policy.

37 This is Blique's term. Blique, *Logical Fallacy Monsters*, 104–5.

Chapter 9: Writing about Anything

1 Zakaria, *Liberal Education*, 72. See also Raab, *Who Is the Historian?*, 101.

2 Berkin and Anderson, *History Handbook*, 79.

3 Jennifer Hess, "BY328 Guidelines for Laboratory Manuscripts" (handout, Aquinas College, Spring 2019).

4 Berkin and Anderson, *History Handbook*, 78.

5 Marius and Page, *Short Guide*, 119–20.

6 Hess, "BY328 Guidelines."

7 Raab, *Who Is the Historian?*, 101.

8 Keith Coffman, "CNN Hit with $275 Million Defamation Suit by
Kentucky Student," Reuters, March 12, 2019, https://www.reuters.com
/article/us-usa-nativeamerican/cnn-hit-with-275-million-defamation
-suit-by-kentucky-student-idUSKBN1QU0BY; Sarah Brookbank, "Nick
Sandmann: Covington Catholic Student's Legal Team Sues NBC, MSNBC
for $275M," *USA Today*, May 2, 2019, https://www.usatoday.com/story
/news/nation/2019/05/02/covington-catholic-nick-sandmann-legal-team
-sues-nbc-msnbc/3649837002/; CNN Staff, "CNN Served with Sandmann
Lawsuit," CNN, March 21, 2019, https://www.cnn.com/2019/03/21/us
/cnn-sandmann-lawsuit/.

SELECT BIBLIOGRAPHY

Arnold, John. *History: A Very Short Introduction*. New York: Oxford University Press, 2000.

Ball, James. *Post-Truth: How Bullshit Conquered the World*. London: Biteback, 2017.

Berkin, Carol, and Betty S. Anderson. *The History Handbook*. 2nd ed. Boston: Wadsworth Cengage Learning, 2012.

Blique. *Logical Fallacy Monsters: An Illustrated Collection of Logical Fallacies*. Self-published, CreateSpace, 2017.

Chaffee, John. *Thinking Critically*. 6th ed. Boston: Houghton Mifflin, 2000.

Cooke, Nicole A. *Fake News and Alternative Facts: Information Literacy in a Post-Truth Era*. Chicago: ALA Editions, 2018.

"The CRAAP Test." Meriam Library, California State University, Chico. Last updated September 2, 2020. http://libguides.csuchico.edu/Literature Reviews?p=2822716.

"Evaluating Information: Home." American Library Association. Last updated March 18, 2019. http://libguides.ala.org/InformationEvaluation.

"Fact Checking, Verification & Fake News: Fact-Checking Your Reporting." Craig Newmark Graduate School of Journalism at the City University of New York. Last updated August 25, 2020. https://researchguides .journalism.cuny.edu/c.php?g=547454&p=4256107.

Fea, John. *Why Study History? Reflection on the Importance of the Past*. Grand Rapids, MI: Baker Academic, 2013.

Fischer, David Hackett. *Historians' Fallacies: Toward a Logic of Historical Thought*. New York: Harper Torchbooks, 1970.

Gaddis, John Lewis. *The Landscape of History: How Historians Map the Past*. Oxford: Oxford University Press, 2004.

Gula, Robert J. *Nonsense: Red Herrings, Straw Men and Sacred Cows: How We Abuse Logic in Our Everyday Language*. Mount Jackson, VA: Axios, 2007.

Harris, Robert. "Evaluating Internet Research Sources." VirtualSalt. Last modified October 11, 2018. https://www.virtualsalt.com/evalu8it.htm.

Hartley, Scott. *The Fuzzy and the Techie: Why the Liberal Arts Will Rule the Digital World*. Boston: Houghton Mifflin Harcourt, 2017.

Hurley, Patrick J., *A Concise Introduction to Logic*. 9th ed. Belmont, CA: Wadsworth, 2006.

Jordanova, Ludmilla. *History in Practice*. 2nd ed. London: Hodder Education, 2006.

Kelly, T. Mills. *Teaching History in the Digital Age*. Ann Arbor: University of Michigan Press, 2016.

Loughran, Tracey, ed. *A Practical Guide to Studying History: Skills and Approaches*. London: Bloomsbury, 2017.

Maloy, Robert, and Allison Malinowski. *Wiki Works: Teaching Web Research and Digital Literacy in History and Humanities Classrooms*. Lanham, MD: Rowman & Littlefield, 2017.

Marius, Richard, and Melvin E. Page. *A Short Guide to Writing about History*. 8th ed. New York: Pearson, 2012.

Novick, Peter. *That Noble Dream: The "Objectivity Question" and the American Historical Profession*. Cambridge: Cambridge University Press, 1988.

Pariser, Eli. *The Filter Bubble: How the New Personalized Web Is Changing What We Read and How We Think*. New York: Penguin Books, 2011.

Passmore, Kevin. "Evidence and Interpretation." In *A Practical Guide to Studying History: Skills and Approaches*, edited by Tracey Loughran, 139–54. London: Bloomsbury, 2017.

Phillips, Paul T. *Truth, Morality, and Meaning in History*. Toronto: University of Toronto Press, 2019.

Postman, Neil. *Technopoly: The Surrender of Culture to Technology*. New York: Vintage Books, 1993.

Presnell, Jenny L. *The Information-Literate Historian: A Guide to Research for History Students*. 3rd ed. Oxford: Oxford University Press, 2019.

Raab, Nigel A. *Who Is the Historian?* Toronto: University of Toronto Press, 2016.

Rampolla, Mary Lynn. *A Pocket Guide to Writing in History*. 8th ed. Boston: Bedford/St. Martin's, 2015.

Roche, Mark. *Why Choose the Liberal Arts?* Notre Dame, IN: University of Notre Dame Press, 2010.

Stebbins, Leslie F. *Student Guide to Research in the Digital Age*. Westport, CT: Libraries Unlimited, 2005.

Storey, William Kelleher. *Writing History: A Guide for Students*. 5th ed. Oxford: Oxford University Press, 2016.

Stross, Randall. *A Practical Education: Why Liberal Arts Majors Make Great Employees*. Stanford: Stanford University Press, 2017.

Trueman, Carl. *Histories and Fallacies: Problems Faced in the Writing of History*. Wheaton, IL: Crossway, 2010.

Van Vleet, Jacob E. *Informal Logical Fallacies: A Brief Guide*. New York: University Press of America, 2011.

Walton, Douglas. *Informal Fallacies: Towards a Theory of Argument of Criticisms.*
    Philadelphia: John Benjamins, 1987. ProQuest Ebook Central.
Wineburg, Sam. "Why Historical Thinking Is Not about History." *History
    News* (Spring 2016): 13–16.
Wineburg, Sam, Sarah McGrew, Joel Breakstone, and Teresa Ortega.
    "Evaluating Information: The Cornerstone of Civic Online Reasoning."
    Stanford Digital Repository. 2016. http://purl.stanford.edu/fv751yt5934.
Zakaria, Fareed. *In Defense of a Liberal Education.* New York: W.W. Norton &
    Company, 2015.

INDEX

Page numbers in italics represent figures/images.